MONTANA'S STATE CAPITOL

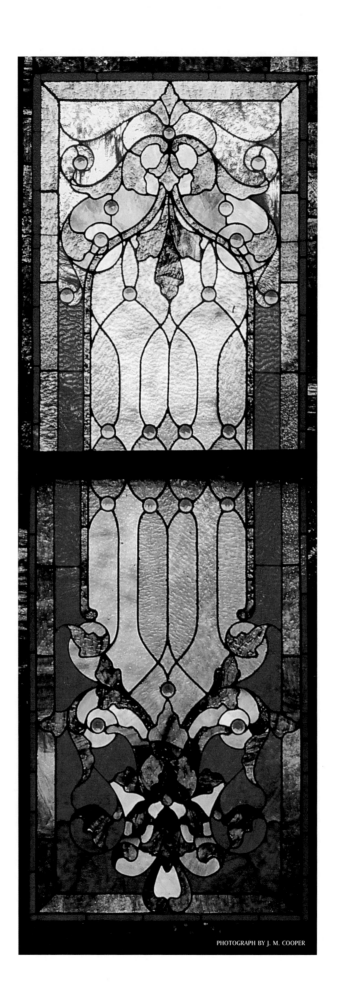

MONTANA'S
STATE CAPITOL

THE PEOPLE'S HOUSE

KIRBY LAMBERT

PATRICIA M. BURNHAM

SUSAN R. NEAR

Kirby Lambert
Patricia M. Burnham
Susan R. Near

MONTANA
HISTORICAL
SOCIETY
PRESS

HELENA

COVER DESIGN Kathryn Fehlig
BOOK DESIGN Arrow Graphics, Missoula
TYPESET IN Sabon and Amerigo

PRINTED BY
Friesens, Altona, Manitoba

FRONT COVER
Capitol at Night, by Clay Schulz, 2000, photographed by John Reddy

BACK COVER
Interior of the Capitol Dome, 2001, photographed by Tom Ferris

Photographs of the Rotunda on page v were taken by Tom Ferris and used courtesy of the photographer.
Photographs on pages 27 and 35 were used courtesy of the photographer George Lane. All other
photographs are from the collections of the Montana Historical Society, Helena.

02 03 04 05 06 07 08 09 10   11 10 9 8 7 6 5 4 3 2 1

ISBN 0-917298-83-7

PRINTED IN CANADA

LIBRARY OF CONGRESS CATALOGING-IN-PUBLICATION DATA

Lambert, Kirby.
    Montana's state capitol : the people's house / Kirby Lambert, Patricia M. Burnham,
Susan R. Near.
        p. cm.
    Includes index.
    ISBN 0-917298-83-7
    1. Montana State Capitol (Helena, Mont.) 2. Helena (Mont.)—Buildings, structures, etc.
I. Burnham, Patricia Mullan, 1935– II. Near, Susan R. III. Title.

NA4412.M9 L36 2002
725'.11'09786615—dc21   2002019605

Funding for *Montana's State Capitol: The People's House*
was provided by the Montana History Foundation.

MHF

MONTANA HISTORY
FOUNDATION

PHOTOGRAPH BY TOM FERRIS

CONTENTS

ARTWORK IN THE MONTANA STATE CAPITOL
SECOND FLOOR

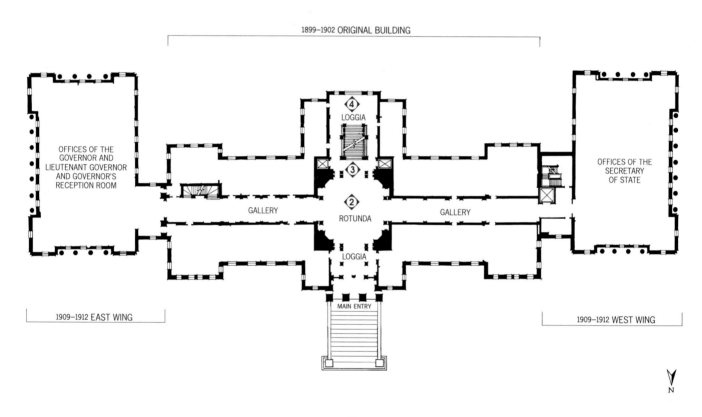

1899–1902 ORIGINAL BUILDING

OFFICES OF THE GOVERNOR AND LIEUTENANT GOVERNOR AND GOVERNOR'S RECEPTION ROOM

④ LOGGIA

③

② ROTUNDA

GALLERY

GALLERY

LOGGIA

MAIN ENTRY

OFFICES OF THE SECRETARY OF STATE

1909–1912 EAST WING

1909–1912 WEST WING

N

①

KEY

① Meagher Statue

② Pedretti Roundels; Walsh, Wheeler, and Dixon Busts

③ Grand Stairway and Barrel Vault

④ Rankin Statue

Map adapted from James P. McDonald, *Historic Structure Report: Montana State Capitol Building* (Helena: State of Montana, Architectural/Engineering Office, 1981): 198

viii

ARTWORK IN THE MONTANA STATE CAPITOL
THIRD FLOOR

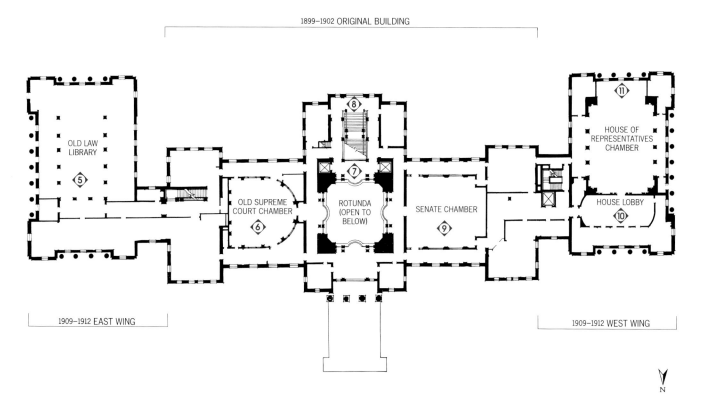

1899–1902 ORIGINAL BUILDING

OLD LAW LIBRARY
5

OLD SUPREME COURT CHAMBER
6

ROTUNDA (OPEN TO BELOW)
7

8

SENATE CHAMBER
9

HOUSE OF REPRESENTATIVES CHAMBER
11

HOUSE LOBBY
10

1909–1912 EAST WING

1909–1912 WEST WING

N

KEY

5 DeCamp Murals

6 Pedretti Murals

7 Mansfield Statue

8 Joullin Mural

9 Pedretti Murals

10 Paxson Murals

11 Russell Mural

NOTE: Sanders Statue location TBA;
Liberty Statue atop dome

Map adapted from James P. McDonald, *Historic Structure Report: Montana State Capitol Building* (Helena: State of Montana, Architectural/Engineering Office, 1981): 248

The
HISTORY

BUILDING THE CAPITOL

KIRBY LAMBERT

*[The Capitol] will be to the state what the
homestead is to the citizen, what
the fireside is to the family. . . . Here
should repose the honor and conscience
of the state by which its citizenship
shall be judged and measured and its
glory achieved and preserved.*

GOVERNOR JOSEPH K. TOOLE
JULY 4, 1899

SINCE 1902 THE Montana State Capitol has stood as both a commanding symbol of the past and a bold promise for the future. Planned and constructed during the two decades following Montana's admission to the Union, the building stands as a tangible declaration of the values and aspirations of Montana's founders. At its most fundamental level, of course, the Capitol serves as a necessary home for the physical workings of state government. Just as important, however, is the symbolic role this historically and architecturally significant structure plays in the lives of the Treasure State's citizens. It is Montana's "temple of democracy," a monumental showplace that embodies egalitarian ideals in art and architecture befitting both the state's proud heritage and our forebears' hope for a bright future.

THE CAPITOL'S STORY begins almost forty years before its construction, as its early history is interwoven into the larger tale of a young territory's quest for statehood. Although the creation of such an edifice was undoubtedly far from the minds of the first trappers, traders, and prospectors who entered the region, statehood, and the consequent need for a statehouse, was an overriding concern for many who followed. When Montana became a territory in May 1864, the mining camp of Bannack—the site of the Treasure State's first significant gold rush—was selected as the seat of government. Far removed from the amenities that characterized eastern capitals, lawmakers scrambled for meeting space when Montana's First Territorial Legislature convened that December. The seven-member Upper Council met in a single-story log structure while the thirteen-member Lower House gathered in a similar, two-story building nearby.

Bannack's tenure as Montana's capital and premiere gold camp, however, was short lived. By the time the legislature assembled in Bannack, richer gold deposits had been found in Alder Gulch, fifty miles to the east. Many miners had already abandoned Bannack in favor of Virginia City, a boomtown flourishing in Alder Gulch.

Montana's First Territorial Legislature assembled in Bannack in December 1864 to enact "such laws as may conduce to the happiness and prosperity of the people." This photograph, taken long after Bannack's heyday, depicts one of the buildings in which that legislature assembled.

Following suit, the legislature voted to relocate, and early in 1865, the capital was moved. As in Bannack, Montana's government situated itself wherever space could be found. Over the next ten years, a variety of Virginia City buildings provided homes for the legislature and various territorial offices.

Like Bannack, Virginia City's status as territorial capital depended on the eminence of its gold deposits, and by 1867 another camp, Helena, was challenging Virginia City in both arenas. Located ninety miles north of Alder Gulch, Helena traced its beginnings to 1864 when four weary prospectors —known to history as the "Four Georgians," although only one was actually from that state—decided to make one last attempt before giving up their search for gold. Their final effort yielded a bonanza, and the locale was christened Last Chance Gulch in recognition of the prospectors' perseverance.

Changing its name from Last Chance Gulch to the more dignified Helena, the "Queen City" soon began to vie for the title of territorial capital. At Helena's instigation, referendums were called in 1867 and 1869 to choose the seat of government. Both favored Virginia City, although allegations of corruption marred the 1869 contest. Political shenanigans were so pervasive during a third referendum held in 1874 that the territory's Supreme Court was forced to intervene. It ultimately declared Helena the winner, and in

BELOW: The second floor of this commercial building, photographed about 1868, was one of several Virginia City facilities that housed Montana's territorial government between 1865 and 1875.

Helena's Main Street, circa 1879, as it appeared shortly after the "Queen City" became Montana's territorial capital.

spring 1875 Montana's territorial government moved for a second time. On April 8, Virginia City's *Weekly Montanian* reported, "Some of the numerous wagons of the Diamond R arrived here on Monday last. The law library of the Territory, and papers and archives belonging to the office of the Secretary, were packed up and placed in the prairie schooners. . . . Col. Callaway, the Territorial Secretary . . . will leave town in about a week to look after the property of the government which is now on wheels."

Upon arriving in Helena, the government offices once again made do with available space. Upon completion of the new Lewis and Clark County Courthouse in 1887, however, Montana's territorial government moved into the majestic Romanesque structure, then one of the most commanding buildings in the territory. After Montana was admitted to the Union in 1889, the newly formed state government remained in the court-house on an interim basis. All together, the building would fill its dual role as statehouse and courthouse for fifteen years.

CERTAIN THAT STATEHOOD would "break the shackles of territorial bondage" and elevate them "to the full dignity of American citizenship," residents of Montana Territory heralded Montana's entrance into the Union on November 8, 1889, as the nation's forty-first state.[1] Among the many tasks involved in transforming a territorial administration into a state government was the selection of a permanent capital. Rather than run the political risks inherent in choosing a site themselves, members of the state's Second Legislative Assembly called for a referendum to let

1. Kenneth N. Owens, "The Prizes of Statehood," *Montana The Magazine of Western History* 37 (Autumn 1987): 2.

the people decide. Seven Montana cities gained a place on the November 1892 ballot—Anaconda, Boulder, Bozeman, Butte, Deer Lodge, Great Falls, and Helena. The initial contest, however, proved inconclusive. Helena and Anaconda led the ballot, but neither obtained a clear majority. The 1891 legislature had stipulated that, in the case of such an event, a runoff would be held during the next general election.

Thus began one of the most vitriolic contests in Montana history, exacerbated by an ongoing feud between Montana's famed "Copper Kings" —Marcus Daly, who backed his own smelting town of Anaconda, and William A. Clark of Butte, who championed Helena, primarily to thwart Daly. Newspapers across the Treasure State joined the fray, verbosely promoting one community while adamantly condemning the other, and "Anaconda-for-Capital" and "Helena-for-Capital" clubs sprang up in all towns of any size.

Anaconda's supporters portrayed Helena as a center of avarice and elitism while promoting their choice as the pick of the workingman. As one flyer proclaimed, "Anaconda is the home of plain people. . . . It is not the ambition of Anaconda to get [a] reputation as a city of snobs." In return, Helena's backers claimed that if the victory should go to their opponent the entire state would be strangled by the "copper collar" of Daly's Anaconda Copper Mining Company. As Helena Reverend J. H. Crooker extolled, "the one great thing which we are called upon to do with all our might at this particular moment is to overthrow the dark design of that giant corporation, which is in the field against our liberties and the prosperity of the state. . . . It is not one town against another, but a corporation against the Commonwealth."

Between 1887 and 1902, most functions of Montana government—first territorial and, later, state—were housed in Helena's Lewis and Clark County Courthouse, pictured here shortly after construction was completed in 1887.

	Helena	Anaconda
Men who wear silk hats	2,625	3
Men who wear No. 7 shoes...........	2,110	5
Men who wear No. 9 shoes...........	2	3,618
Men who wear silk night shirts.......	2,910	4
Men who wear cotton night shirts....	186	3,016
Men who wear kid gloves.............	4,552	4
Men who wear overalls	0	3,220
Patches on seats of trousers.........	1	7
Patches on knees of trousers.........	0	253
Patches on conscience...............	1,691	8
Dinner buckets in daily use	2	4,028
Manhattan cocktails, daily consumption....	17,699	127
Gin fizzes, daily consumption........	18,123	180
Whiskey straights, daily consumption	13,303	1,977
Champagne (qts.), " "	1,245	2
Beers............ " "	4,088	8,854
Ladies who nurse their own babies...	124	2,876
Ladies who do their own washing....	8	980
Ladies who dance the minuet........	3,773	82
Ladies who do the skirt dance.......	861	1
Ladies who can kick the chandelier..	140	0
Ladies with poodle dogs.............	774	0
Ladies with pug dogs................	2,285	3
Ladies with no dogs at all...........	1,863	3,555
Ladies who give high fives..........	2,731	9
Ladies who rip other ladies up the back......	1,296	147
Babies born with silver spoons in mouth......	435	0
Children with Shetland ponies........	590	0
Children who make mud pies.........	0	2,773
Average number children per family	½	5
Horses with docked tails.............	1,182	0
Four-in-hand turnouts....	112	0
Yellow donkey carts.................	215	1
Skeletons in closets.................	1,343	16
People who eat dinner at 6 o'clock....	8,658	456
People who eat dinner at 12 o'clock...	370	6,954

During the 1894 capital fight, *Helena's Social Supremacy*—an anonymously produced pamphlet—satirized the Queen City's reputation for snobbery in an effort to win support for the rival Anaconda.

The election was held November 6, 1894. The contest remained close, but when the final vote was tallied, Helena had narrowly defeated Anaconda. In blaring headlines, the Helena *Herald* proclaimed, "The Capital Stays Here, Boodle and Bossism Rebuked at the Polls by our Patriotic People." Although spontaneous celebrations erupted as soon as the results were known, the city postponed its official "jollification" one week to give Helenans time to prepare and out-of-town supporters an opportunity to travel to their new capital. As a result, November 12, according to the *Herald*, proved to be "the greatest day Montana ever saw in the way of popular rejoicing and demonstration. . . . Never did the sun shine upon a city more given over to the spirit of carnival." Brass bands, drum corps, firecrackers, and cheering throngs greeted the celebrants who arrived throughout the day by train, farm wagon, and stagecoach. That night,

as a full moon soared into the eastern sky, a "monster torchlight procession" capped the day's festivities.

WITH THE VOLATILE capital question officially settled, the lawmakers who gathered in Helena in January 1895 were at last able to turn their attention to securing an appropriate building to house the fledgling state's government. For thirty years, they had made do. Now Montanans wanted a genuine Capitol—not only for the practical benefits gained by facilitating the work of government, but, more importantly, for its symbolic presence. To the citizens of Montana, the anticipated Capitol represented a physical manifestation of statehood. They wanted a building that would express the young "state's ambitions and its commitment to democracy . . . [and] symbolize Montana's acceptance of the cultural and political values of America."[2]

First, of course, the state needed to acquire land upon which to situate its statehouse. Consequently, the legislature appointed a five-member Capitol Site Commission to secure an appropriate tract "of land in a compact body . . . with an area of not less than five, nor more than 30 acres." The Commission called for bids and invited interested citizens to testify at a series of hearings held throughout the summer. The unified front that Helenans had presented in their fight against Anaconda deteriorated rapidly as competing factions appeared before the Commission to voice their opinions. While many advocated for the selection of a central location, the choice ultimately evolved into a west-side versus east-side rivalry.

West-siders backed what they called the "Capitol Hill" site (on what is today the Carroll College campus), a ten-acre parcel owned by noted businessman and politician Samuel T. Hauser. Capitol Hill's proponents lauded it as perfectly situated between Helena's central busi-

2. Carroll Van West, "A Landscape of Statehood: The Montana State Capitol," *Montana The Magazine of Western History* 37 (Autumn 1987): 73.

ness district and "the principal attractions of the city"—including the Broadwater Hotel, Fort Harrison, and Central Park. In contrast, they decried the remoteness of an east-side site. Hauser offered to donate half the acreage to the state, contingent upon the purchase of the other half for ten thousand dollars.

East-side boosters countered with a seventeen-acre tract named after real estate developer and insurance agent Peter Winne, the site's chief proponent. With the highest elevation "of any desirable site offered . . . the view of the surrounding country from this point is excellent," Winne enthusiasts proclaimed, "and a building placed there can be seen from nearly all parts of the City." Asserting that the prosperous west side had more than its share of development, they also argued that the Winne site was "at least 10 degrees warmer in the winter than the principal west side sites." Most importantly, however, the seventeen acres were not only being offered for free, but came with a promise of four thousand dollars in donated funds to be used to help beautify the grounds or defray other expenses.

After three months of impassioned debate, the Capitol Site Commission announced its decision in favor of the Winne site on August 30, 1895. As the Helena *Herald* reported the following day:

> It was the east siders' turn to celebrate last evening and they did not miss the opportunity. . . . A huge bonfire was built right in the center of the capitol tract . . . [and] there were easily over a thousand people who visited the site. . . . It was the choice of the common people without question. The wealthy wanted the capitol on the west side, which already has more than its share of valuable improvements, and the *Herald* is gratified that the business and residence balance of the city has been maintained by giving the capitol to the east side.

With the work of the Capitol Site Commission completed, a second group—the Capitol Commission—assumed control of the construction project. Directed by the legislature to obtain "plans and designs appropriate to a capitol building . . . [and to] secure the erection and completion of said Capitol Building," the Commission had final say in all matters not otherwise mandated by the legislature. The committee was to consist of five members, including the governor, John E. Rickards, who served as chairman, and "four qualified electors." No more than three of its members could belong to any one political party, only one member could be from Helena, and no more than two could be residents of the same county. Members could not in any way profit from the building's construction—violation of this statute would be a felony.

The commissioners' first task was to develop a detailed list of what features they wanted the new Capitol to contain. Accordingly, they produced a proposal that called for a one-hundred-room building that included adequate assembly space for a twenty-three-member Senate and seventy-five-member House of Representatives. In addition, they stipulated that the edifice—which by law could not exceed a cost of one million dollars—should achieve "the highest degree of architectural beauty and constructive excellence." Furthermore, the building was to be fireproof, constructed as far as practicable of native Montana materials, equipped with "the most improved methods of heating, draining, and ventilation," and contain two electric elevators that would "go to all floors."

The Commission advertised for bids not only across Montana, but also in New York, Chicago, St. Louis, and San Francisco and in national trade journals. As a result, fifty-nine architects submitted drawings. Believing that they needed the assistance of an impartial advisor, the Commission hired Seymour Davis, an "Expert Architect" with ties to Philadelphia and Topeka, Kansas, to guide them through the selection process. Following Davis's recommendation, the Commission chose the plan of George R. Mann of St. Louis, Missouri, whose design, according to Davis, was "the best that has been submitted, showing a praiseworthy arrangement throughout." Mann's drawings called for a four-story, 126,000-square-foot edifice that boasted a towering central dome flanked by lower domes capping the House and Senate on either end. When submitting his design, Mann stated that his plan would "reflect by its dignity and monumental effect the power and resources of the great state [of Montana] . . . and also give an arrangement of offices that is practical and convenient."

Following his appointment as the architect of the new Capitol, Mann spent the next several months completing the detailed drawings and specifications that would be needed to guide construction while the Commission turned its attention to the task of financing the building. As part of the Enabling Act that paved the way for Montana's admission to the Union, Congress had granted the state 182,000 acres of federal land intended to back bonds to be sold to fund the Capitol's construction. Selling the bonds proved difficult, however, as low interest rates and other complicating factors diminished the market. Montana's experience was not unique— across the country, other states, and even the federal government, were having limited success disposing of similar bonds.

As problematic for the state as the lack of a market for its bonds was the "uniquely autonomous" nature of the Capitol Commission. Since the monies administered by the commissioners did not originate from the state's general fund, their expenditures fell outside the jurisdiction of the Board of Examiners, which normally audited all state spending. Free from this board's control, nothing prohibited the Commission from appropriating more money than it had, as exemplified by its commitment to erecting a million-dollar building when it held less than ten thousand dollars in actual funds. The situation was precarious because "while the state was not liable for the commission's debts . . . the state's credit was nonetheless at stake."[3] When State Auditor A. B. Cook refused to honor a commissioner's claim that had been presented to him without the Board of Examiners' approval, the issue came to a head. The case ultimately appeared before the Montana Supreme Court where the independent status of the Capitol Commission was upheld, thus allowing the Commission to carry on its activities without the usual checks and balances.

WITH FINAL PLANS in hand, funding problems far from settled, and the Commission's autonomy intact, ground-breaking ceremonies for the Capitol were held on September 10, 1896, a little more than one year after Mann had been selected to design the building. That fall, work crews began excavating the basement and grading nearby streets, eventually lowering Sixth Avenue to ensure that the new statehouse would be shown to its best advantage. As winter weather forced work to a seasonal halt, however, troubling circumstances would soon bring an unexpected end to the existing plans for Montana's long-anticipated Capitol.

In January 1897, the inauguration of Governor Robert B. Smith placed a new chairman at the head of the Capitol Commission. More significantly, however, the Fifth Legislative Assembly also brought to Helena Fred Whiteside, a representative from Flathead County. Upon his arrival in the capital city, the freshman Democrat "caught the odor of various forms of graft" and accused the commissioners of scheming to scam money from the building project and place it in their own pockets. A legislative committee was formed to look into these claims, but—with the exception of Whiteside—the investigative team was composed entirely of those friendly toward the Commission. Not surprisingly, therefore, the investigators found "absolutely no evidence . . . to show any wrongful act upon the part of any member of the Capitol Commission." Whiteside wrote a dissenting report, and to retaliate, members of the Commission unsuccessfully sued the Flathead County legislator for libel.

The upheaval caused by Whiteside's continuing allegations ultimately led to a grand jury

3. James P. McDonald, *Historic Structure Report: Montana State Capitol Building* (Helena: State of Montana, Architectural/ Engineering Office, 1981): 13.

investigation. After collecting "twenty-seven folios of testimony," the grand jury identified its key witness as John C. Paulsen, a Helena architect who had served as Whiteside's primary informant. To convict members of the Commission, however, Paulsen would also have to indict himself for his involvement in similar schemes related to other state building projects. The night before the architect was to testify he died unexpectedly and suspiciously. Newspapers reported the cause of death as apoplexy brought on by "nervous prostration," but many involved in the case believed that the architect had taken his own life in order to avoid the embarrassment of his pending exposure.

With the loss of Paulsen's testimony, the grand jury did not have a case. On April 29, 1897, the headline in the Helena *Weekly Herald* announced, "No Doubt That There Was Crooked Work but Sufficient Evidence Could Not Be Obtained. Important Evidence Lost by Death of Architect Paulsen." The accompanying front-page article explained that "the report commends the conduct of [Commission member] W. K. Flowerree at all times, but otherwise finds that . . . several members of the state capitol commission have been untrue to the duties imposed on them by law. . . . The evidence submitted 'fully corroborates the statements contained in the minority report of Representative Whiteside.'"

ALTHOUGH NONE OF those involved was ever criminally prosecuted, the scandal did have internal repercussions. As suspicions deepened, Governor Smith asked the implicated commissioners to resign. When they refused, he removed them and appointed new Commission members. Also, at the governor's urging and further spurred by worsening economic conditions, the assembled lawmakers of the Fifth Legislative Assembly repealed the earlier legislation that called for the erection of a one-million-dollar building and in its stead appropriated $350,000 to fund the Capitol—a meager sum, even by the standards of the day.

Since the legislature now mandated that the new Capitol be built at one-third the initial cost, Mann's original plans were no longer usable. Instead, the Commission sought to build a smaller structure designed "upon such a plan as will admit of additions thereto, when in the future the needs of the State may require the same." Although Mann initially attempted to modify his original design to meet the new stipulation, he soon asked to be released from the project. The Commission responded by placing all design considerations on hold.

Even though the amount now needed was considerably less than the original one million dollars, the new commissioners still faced the same funding problem that had plagued their predecessors—that of selling bonds that no one wanted to buy. The low interest rates borne by the bonds, the fact that the state was not guaranteeing the bonds, and the actuality that only a small portion of the acreage used to back the bonds had been selected and surveyed all combined to hamper sales. Then, in April 1897, the problem was solved almost effortlessly when Thomas Cruse—a philanthropic mining magnate and Helena banker, who would later donate money to help construct the Cathedral of St. Helena—offered to purchase the entire bond issue. As soon as negotiations were completed and contracts signed, Montana had the money for a new Capitol.

After several months of silence, the Commission reconvened in January 1898 to prepare a new request for architectural bids. Taking into account the realities of the more modest budget, the commissioners now called for a sixty-five-room structure that would include chambers for a twenty-four-member Senate and a sixty-eight-member House of Representatives, with provisions to be made for increasing those bodies to forty and one hundred respectively. A number of firms, including George Mann's, responded. On February 8, 1898, the competing architects were invited to present their plans before the Commission. Shortly thereafter, the commissioners settled on a design prepared by

Architect John H. Kent pictured a bustling political center in his rendering of the proposed Montana Capitol, circa 1898. Upon the completion of the structure four years later, Montana's Capitol Commission justified the cost of construction by describing the building as "its own best argument."

the architectural firm of Charles E. Bell and John H. Kent.

At the time they submitted their bid, Bell and Kent were situated in Council Bluffs, Iowa, but before the Commission's selection was publicly announced in March, the partners relocated to Helena to meet the legislature's demand that the architect of the Capitol be a resident of the state. Bell, who early in his career had worked both as a carpenter and a public building inspector, "brought a builder's eye to the Montana capitol project."[4] Before joining in partnership with Bell in 1894, Kent had worked for two years with Detroit architect Elijah E. Myers, who has been described as "the greatest capitol-builder of the Gilded Age."[5] Together, the two had a solid reputation in the Midwest as designers of public buildings, including courthouses, schools, and business blocks. During their tenure in Montana, Bell and Kent designed a number of other buildings around the state, most notably the Deer Lodge County Courthouse in Anaconda, the Flathead County Courthouse in Kalispell, the public school at Columbus, the Hotel Havre in Havre, and several business blocks in Glasgow.

Stylistically, Bell and Kent's design for the Montana statehouse adhered to the tenets of the architectural movement known as the American Renaissance. Originating on the east coast in the 1880s, this neoclassic revival reinterpreted the aesthetics of ancient Greece and Rome in an effort to substantiate the United States' role as "a powerful nation that would perpetuate the best of western civilization and culture."[6] Especially suited to large-scale public buildings in both form and ideology, American Renaissance architecture was showcased at Chicago's World's Columbian Exposition in

4. Van West, "A Landscape of Statehood," 74.

5. Henry-Russell Hitchcock and William Seale, *Temples of Democracy: The State Capitols of the USA* (New York: Harcourt Brace Jovanovich, 1976): 174.

6. Van West, "A Landscape of Statehood," 75.

The cornerstone for the new Capitol was dedicated with great fanfare on July 4, 1899. The erection of the imposing structure further cemented Helena's claim as Montana's capital, making it highly unlikely that a referendum put to the voters would ever succeed in removing the title to another community.

11

1893, where a model "White City" brought the style to the attention of the entire nation. Thereafter, according to noted architectural historians Henry-Russell Hitchcock and William Seale, "no capitol in the United States went unaffected by the American Renaissance," and Bell and Kent's Montana design represented "a good example of the way the high style was revised far from the national centers. . . . [It was] a mountain state's version of the Eastern Renaissance."[7]

UPON APPROVING THE architects' final plans in July 1898, the Commission began searching for a firm to construct the building. After reviewing the ten bids received, in September they awarded the contract to Joseph Soss of Butte for $289,891. Shortly thereafter Soss, with the Commission's approval, transferred the contract to the newly formed Montana Building Com-

pany, of which H. L. Frank, a well-known citizen and former mayor of Butte, was president. Soss, in turn, was employed as the company's general manager.

Work began immediately. After refilling part of the excavation that had been prepared for Mann's larger building, crews completed the foundation that fall. The Commission turned its attention to selecting the stone that would be used to face the building, and over the winter, commissioners visited quarries in Ulm, Great Falls, and Billings before choosing sandstone from a Columbus quarry, which they found ample in quantity, "uniform in color and free from defects." The next spring, commissioners hired a superintendent of construction, J. A. Murphy of Helena, to oversee progress and ensure that the State's interests were met throughout the project.

7. Hitchcock and Seale, *Temples of Democracy*, 226, 229–30.

With work well underway, in May 1899 the Commission began planning a celebration to mark the laying of the building's cornerstone. They directed Bell and Kent to design an appropriate stone adorned with the State Seal on its north face and the date of the ceremony, July 4, 1899, on its west face. In addition, a Committee on Archives, appointed by the governor, selected items to be placed in a "metallic box within the stone." The Committee filled the time capsule with a variety of mementos significant to Montana history, including an 1870 photograph of the Helena's Hangman's Tree, a copy of Thomas Dimsdale's *The Vigilantes of Montana*, and a piece of adobe brick from old Fort Benton.

On July 4, Helena overflowed with celebrants arriving from all corners of the state. A grand Masonic procession, music, and speeches highlighted the festivities. In his address to the gathered crowds, former governor Joseph K. Toole summarized the day's foremost sentiment when he proclaimed, "From that supreme hour when we laid away forever our territorial robes and donned the 'stately stoles' of sovereignty to this glad day, we have looked forward with increasing pride and abiding interest to the time when construction of the State Capitol would be inaugurated."

ALTHOUGH THE LEGISLATURE had originally called for the completion of the building by January 1, 1900, the setbacks that had already occurred and the delays inherent in any project of this scope combined to push the deadline back. It would take an additional three years after the cornerstone was laid to complete the building. Initially, the Commission carried on its work under the direction of Governor Smith. The elections of 1900, however, delivered a new governor to Montana, and correspondingly, a new head to the Capitol Commission. That governor, Joseph K. Toole, previously had served as the first governor of Montana from 1889 to 1892. When he resumed the governorship in January 1901, he brought to the Capitol Commission an enthusiasm unmatched by his predecessors. With his passion, however, came a desire to control all decisions of any import to the building's final appearance.

Increasingly, as construction progressed, the project was marked by strained relationships between the Commission and the Montana Building Company. Tension culminated in March 1901 with Soss's resignation as general manager. But Soss was not the only one to have differences with the Commission. In July, Toole and his fellow Commission members determined that Kent's low, spherical "Flathead Indian dome" represented "an unnecessary concession to frugality."[8] Against Kent's wishes, but backed by Bell, they insisted that the dome be raised, thus achieving a higher, more imposing structure with relatively little added expense. Kent later lamented, "There is only one difference between the original design and the completed building, and that is the shape of the dome. . . . I made my design as far as possible pure Greek, dignified and reposeful, but the Commission, backed by my late partner, induced me to raise the Crown of the dome, and so it remains the only really imperfect feature (tho' alas the most prominent one) of an otherwise pretty good looking building."

Although the Capitol was far from finished when lawmakers gathered in Helena in January 1901, enough work had been accomplished "to show them that the structure was to be a credit to the State." Consequently, the legislators appropriated an additional sixty thousand dollars to be used for furnishing the statehouse, a contingency not provided for in the original funding. Supervision of this portion of the project was given to the State Furnishing Board—a standing committee composed of the governor, the secretary of state, and the attorney general.

Of the tasks assigned to the State Furnishing Board, the most notable were the procurement of custom-made furniture and light fixtures based on designs developed by Bell and Kent.

8. McDonald, *Historic Structure Report*, 63.

The architects' original plans called for a low, spherical dome. A last-minute change provided for a taller, more imposing dome, the skeletal iron framework of which is pictured here in 1901.

The contract for the desks and chairs for the House and Senate and other office furniture proved to be the most problematic—Montana's unions protested the Board's initial choice as "hostile to labor" and forced the selection of another manufacturer. It was the choosing of light fixtures, however, that drew the most attention. From the beginning, the use of electric lights (at the time still a noteworthy feature) had been a highly touted element of the architects' design. The selection of appropriate chandeliers and wall sconces was, therefore, crucial.

While the choices made by the Furnishing Board would have tremendous impact on the finished appearance of the building's interior, the decision that would have the most dramatic effect—the selection of a decorating firm to over-see the interior design—was handled not by the State Furnishing Board, but by the Capitol Commission itself. The chosen decorator would have to coordinate all design components including color schemes and the art glass. In addition, the selected firm would be responsible for the feature most essential to the success of the new statehouse's decor—the creation of murals and other decorative painting that would adorn the building's grandest interior spaces. The Commission received bids from seven decorators, and after a careful review of the submitted designs, they narrowed the choice to two out-of-state firms, Crossman and Sturdy of Chicago and F. Pedretti's Sons of Cincinnati. Final deliberations resulted in a three-to-two vote in favor of the Cincinnati firm, and on August 21, 1901, F. Pedretti's Sons was awarded a twenty-five-thousand-dollar contract to decorate the Capitol. No serious consideration had been given to the lone Montana applicant, Charles Schatzlein of Butte, who commissioners doubted had the necessary experience for a project of this scope.

IN JANUARY 1902, after several days of frenzied, last-minute preparations and a thorough inspection by the Commission, the Montana Building Company officially turned the structure over to the State. While the actual construction was now complete, a tremendous amount of finishing work remained. After the Pedretti firm chose a final color scheme in January, successive waves of painters, tile layers, carpet layers, electricians, "frescoers," and stained-glass artists began work inside the building.

With the interior decorating continuing apace, the Capitol Commission turned its attention to the building's surroundings. Seeking to transform the Capitol grounds into a showplace befitting the home of state government, they hired a landscape architect from Chicago to develop a master plan. After receiving the resulting drawings, however, it became evident that funding constraints would allow for only partial implementation of the design. Consequently, the Commission directed that the proposal be "followed or deviated from as may seem best . . . but the general idea should be followed, using as far as practicable, native growth."

The State was assisted in its landscaping efforts by the Helena Improvement Society. Organized in 1898—and dedicated to such betterment projects as removing vagrant cows from the city's streets and transforming Mount Helena into a city park—the Helena Improvement Society

The price tag for Montana's new Capitol—including construction, furnishing, decorating, and landscaping (pictured here)—totaled approximately $540,000.

14

The inclusion of electric lights—like the chandelier and fixtures capping the columns in the Senate—was such an innovative feature that, prior to the building's opening, the Commission hosted nocturnal tours for specially invited dignitaries to showcase the effects of the artificial illumination.

devoted much of its 1902 campaign to enhancing Sixth Avenue, the principal approach from the city's center to the Capitol. At the group's instigation, Sixth Avenue was regraded, water mains were extended to allow for irrigation, and grass and trees were planted between the sidewalks and street, creating the Queen City's first "regularly parked street."

As work inside the Capitol neared completion, the Commission selected the Fourth of July as the date for the building's official dedication. July 4 was chosen in part because it was the earliest date that they could realistically expect the building to be ready. More importantly, however, the nation's birthday was chosen for its meaning to the American people. As United States Senator William A. Clark noted, by dedicating the Capitol on "the anniversary of our

national independence," the state will perpetuate "those very principles which were on that day first formally declared, and afterwards securely founded."

In anticipation of this historic milestone, a reception committee—made up of a host of the state's leading citizens—was established to help prepare for "the largest and most notable assembly of pioneers, politicians, and prominent people ever witnessed in the state." Although plans called for the ceremonies to be held outdoors, July 4 dawned cold and blustery, and at the last moment rain showers drove the festivities inside. Crowds filled "the rotunda, the corridors, the grand stairway and even the balconies of the third and fourth floors—wherever there was standing room." Addressing the assembled throng, Senator Clark elaborated upon the building's significance

The completed statehouse—including the Governor's Reception Room pictured here in 1903—was lauded as "perfect in its appointments, modern in construction, complete in detail, beautiful in appearance, and in all ways satisfactory and desirable."

to the young state by declaring, "In the dedication of this magnificent structure there has been rounded out and completed all the requirements of full-fledged statehood. . . . We are now equipped with all the facilities and conveniences essential to the exercise of all the functions of state government."

The following morning the *Montana Daily Record* decreed that Montana's new statehouse was a "Triumph of Architect and Decorator." The paper attributed this victory to the "severe dignity" of the Capitol's exterior combined with "its highly ornate, rich interior." Decades later, authors Henry-Russell Hitchcock and William Seale supported the *Daily Record*'s initial assessment, agreeing that, in the case of the Capitol's imposing facade, "simplicity here does achieve grandeur."[9]

While the building's exterior owed its "severe dignity" to its American Renaissance styling, the Capitol's opulent interior reflected the aesthetics of an earlier age—here "was the American Renaissance expressed in the language of the Gilded Age."[10] At the urging of Governor Toole, who favored the style because of its symbolic connection to the Louisiana Purchase, F. Pedretti's Sons had decorated the interior according to the florid dictates of the French Renaissance, one of several revival styles popular in the second half of the nineteenth century that took inspiration from the European Renaissance.

9. Hitchcock and Seale, *Temples of Democracy*, 230.
10. Ibid.

The House Chamber, the Senate Chamber, and the Governor's Reception Room all received widespread praise. The upper walls of the House and Senate—which were located on the building's third floor on either side of the Rotunda—were adorned with Pedretti murals depicting scenes from Montana history, the subjects for which had been chosen primarily by Governor Toole. Although the Governor's Reception Room lacked the large-scale history paintings that dominated the legislative chambers, it was finished in "ivory and old rose, with walls in green and panels of red silk velours." As secretary of the Capitol Commission, E. B. Kennedy, reported, "the idea followed in the decorations and furnishings of this room was to give the proper treatment to what might be called the 'State Parlor,' and it has been faithfully carried out in all of its details."

But it was the Rotunda—the "conceptual seat of government in Montana . . . where the axis of the citizens and the axis of their government intersect"—that received the greatest attention, both from those responsible for the building's design and from the admiring public.[11] As a stylistic and symbolic focal point, the Rotunda contained a number of the building's most outstanding features—a grand staircase crowned by an art glass barrel vault; a highly ornamented dome adorned with murals, decorative painting, and art glass windows; scagliola (imitation marble) columns capped by showy electric fixtures; Tennessee marble wainscoting; and a floor of hexagonal glass tiles. Leading away from the Rotunda to the east and west, wide galleries provided perspective and offered visual balance to the Rotunda's soaring dome. And linking all of these features together was the play of light—the highly touted electric lights, the diffused light filtering through the art glass of the barrel vault, and the natural light streaming through the massive windows at the east and west ends of the two galleries.

ALTHOUGH THE NEW Capitol fulfilled strikingly Montanans' need for a symbolic home for their state's government, in a relatively short period

it was found to be lacking from a functional standpoint. Due to funding limitations, the Capitol Commission had intentionally acquired a smaller structure than was really needed, with the view that it could be expanded as necessity demanded. In less than a decade, lack of space in the statehouse had become a critical issue. As the Anaconda *Standard* reported:

> As the state grew each office found its business increasing, records piled up and [the] vault room became utterly inadequate for the needs of the secretary of state, auditor, and treasurer. . . . [There was] no place whatever for the railroad commission, which occupied the quarters of the House of Representatives when the legislature was not in session. When it was in session the commissioners moved to the attic. The Supreme Court room and chambers of the Supreme Court justices never were adequate for the work of the court, and the historical library outgrew the quarters assigned to it in the basement before it had been there a year.

To alleviate the space shortage, in 1909 the Eleventh Legislative Assembly approved an expansion project for the Capitol. The new construction would be funded in the same way that the original building had—through the sale of bonds backed by land granted to Montana at the time of statehood (this time, the State Board of Land commissioners was the sole bidder on the bonds). The total project could not cost more than $500,000. The State Board of Examiners—composed of the governor, the attorney general, and the secretary of state—would function as the Capitol Commission, overseeing all aspects of the venture.

To help them prepare for their new duties, members of the Commission planned a trip east for the "purpose of viewing public buildings and investigating architects, contractors, and materials." Leaving Helena in April, they traveled by train to the capitals of South Dakota, Minnesota, Wisconsin, Indiana, and Kentucky

---

11. McDonald, *Historic Structure Report*, 199.

where they toured an array of statehouses that recently had been completed or soon would be. In South Dakota, commissioners visited a near-replica of the Montana statehouse designed by Charles Bell. In Madison, the delegation toured the six-million-dollar Wisconsin edifice, but it was the two-million-dollar Kentucky Capitol that impressed the travelers as "the best we had seen for the money invested."

Back in Helena, the Commission sought bids for the design of the desired additions, advertising for a plan that would "be proper from an architectural standpoint and of use and benefit to the state for practical purposes." Wanting to choose a more experienced eastern architect but facing political pressure to hire a resident Montanan, the Commission compromised by doing both. The Board queried three well-known out-of-state firms to see if they would be willing to work in conjunction with a Montana associate. Only one, Frank M. Andrews, responded positively. Consequently, in May, after having "duly weighed and thoroughly considered" the six bids received, the Commission chose Andrews's New York firm to design the additions. Andrews, however, would be assisted in his efforts by the Butte firm of Link and Haire.

Frank M. Andrews was a rising New York architect whose work included the Kentucky statehouse that had so impressed the Commission. Charles S. Haire had studied and practiced architecture in his native Ohio before working as a draftsman, initially for the Union Pacific Railroad in Idaho and later the Great Northern Railway in Butte. Following his employment on the Capitol project, he designed other structures for a variety of state institutions in Bozeman, Dillon, and Boulder. German born and trained, John G. Link practiced architecture in Denver and St. Louis before relocating to Butte in 1896. Link was highly regarded across the Treasure State, and among his other notable commissions was the design of the Montana State Building at the Louisiana Purchase Exposition in St. Louis in 1904.

In forming a partnership between the two firms, the Commission created a situation that would eventually—as the other two queried architects had predicted—produce an intolerable working arrangement for Andrews. The Commission stipulated that his New York firm would produce the designs and that Andrews would have "full power and authority to suggest improvement or insist upon the following of plans." For their part, Link and Haire would "take charge of the actual construction," seeing "to the execution of the plan in all particulars." In theory, the Commission would act as an impartial arbitrator should any disagreement arise between the two firms. In practice, however, the Commission almost always sided with the Montana architects, denying Andrews the continued input that he had been guaranteed.

In July, the Commission approved Andrews's preliminary drawings for the expansion. His plans called for the addition of two symmetrical wings—designed to blend architecturally with the original building—to the east and west ends of the existing building. As soon as the plans were approved, the Commission supplied the state's newspapers with "a large picture of the Capitol Building as it will appear when the wings are completed," along with reports detailing the "chief items of interest." The original drawings were exhibited for public inspection in store windows in Butte and Anaconda and at the State Fair in Helena.

THE RELATIVE EASE with which the project began ended abruptly in fall 1909 as a furor erupted over the selection of the stone that was to be used to face the new wings. In authorizing the building addition, the legislature had mandated that Montana materials be used whenever they could be procured at a price comparable to like products originating outside the state. As awarded, the contract called for the use of either Columbus, Montana, sandstone (as used on the original structure) or Bedford, Indiana, limestone selected to "harmonize in color" with the existing sandstone. However, when it became apparent that the Columbus stone would

Although the new wings—shown here under construction in 1910—provided much-needed space, the loss of the large windows at the east and west ends of the original building substantially darkened the Capitol's interior.

cost at least sixty thousand dollars more than the Bedford stone, the builders—the Billings firm of Gagnon and Company—prepared to go with the cheaper, out-of-state material. The Columbus Sandstone Company cried foul, insisting that its stone be used but refusing to lower its price.

Support for the Montana quarry poured in from all quarters. Chambers of Commerce, labor unions, and business owners from across the state bombarded the Commission, demanding the use of native material. Then, rival Montana quarry owners joined the fray, insisting that if a Montana stone was going to be used, they "be permitted to enter into the competition for said work." To further complicate matters, the commissioners found that the sandstone used on

the original structure was not wearing well. They surveyed a wide variety of builders from across the country who agreed that sandstone was unfit for exterior construction in regions where it would be "subject to any considerable variations in temperature." Instead, the builders uniformly recommended the use of either granite—which was harder and therefore more expensive to quarry and work—or Bedford limestone, which was less expensive than granite but "pleasing in appearance" and extremely durable.

The situation escalated, and yielding to the mounting pressure, Governor Edwin L. Norris convened a special session of the legislature on December 27, 1909, to resolve the issue. After four days of debate, the legislature approved a

Montana's statehouse, pictured here about 1918, assumed its present-day configuration with the addition of wings to the east and west ends of the original structure. The granite-faced wings, which were completed in 1912, were constructed and furnished at a cost of $650,000.

compromise that featured neither of the two disputed stones. While lawmakers did endorse the use of an "enduring stone quarried from the Treasure State," they determined that granite, not sandstone, was their stone of choice. Accordingly, they appropriated $150,000 (in addition to the earlier allocation) to pay for the more expensive stone.

In February 1910, the Commission chose a Jefferson County quarry operated by the firm of T. Kain and Sons to supply the estimated 54,000 cubic feet of granite needed for the project. Kain agreed to deliver the granite to the Capitol grounds, cut and ready to set, for the sum of $192,890. Problems persisted, however, since the use of granite, in place of the more workable sand-

stone, required the redesign of some of the more intricate exterior details. The Commission asked Haire to make these changes, but Andrews balked at having another firm tamper with his plans, telegramming the Commission that "such a procedure is unheard of." Andrews submitted his own revisions, but the Commission found them "not in accordance with the contract heretofore entered into with Kain and Sons" and informed the New York architect that they would use Haire's details. Although Andrews continued to protest, the Commission remained "willing, with-

out a qualm, to sacrifice as much of Andrews's 'original design' as they felt necessary."[12]

With a confrontational tone having been established, the remainder of the construction project was marked by antagonism. Progress was much slower than the Commission anticipated. Although Andrews had warned them that the use of granite would slow the job down, the Commission insisted that the original schedule be maintained. When the commissioners reprimanded the

---

12. Ibid., 97–98.

construction company for repeated delays, Gagnon blamed the stonecutters, who in turn faulted the architects and construction superintendent for not supplying the drawings needed to guide their work. The Northern Pacific, Great Northern, and Chicago, Milwaukee, St. Paul and Pacific railroads—which had given reduced freight rates in exchange for a guaranteed percentage of the shipments of needed building materials—complained that the state was not keeping its end of the bargain. Labor troubles, including strikes by both construction crews and stonecutters, twice brought progress to a halt. And the Commission repeatedly proved willing to meddle in minor details that should have been left to the architects and builders.

UNLIKE THE ORIGINAL construction project, which had called upon a second committee to equip the Capitol, this time the Capitol Commission was also responsible for outfitting the new wings. Wherever possible, existing furnishings were to be reused to reduce expenses, but new furnishings still had to be procured. In February 1911, the Commission began extended deliberations regarding the "furniture, electric lights, mantles . . . and decorations . . . and the costs of said" material.

Six murals painted by Ralph Earll DeCamp originally decorated the Law Library, pictured here in 1917. In 1927, the State commissioned four additional landscapes to fill the two central panels on either side of the room.

One of the most significant decisions the Commission faced—and the one that ultimately would offer the greatest benefit for future generations of Montana art enthusiasts—was the selection of an artist, or artists, to create the decorative murals for the new wings. In the short time that had elapsed since the Pedretti firm was chosen to decorate the original building, Montanans' self-confidence had risen to the point that the current Commission was faced with a dilemma its predecessor had not encountered— the demand to employ Montana artists rather than more experienced muralists from out of state. While many felt that the wings should be adorned by classically themed paintings produced by "recognized" eastern artists, others felt strongly that Montanans should be employed to produce murals depicting Montana subjects. As Helena landscape painter Ralph E. DeCamp observed, "the capitol belongs to the people and . . . the average person would be much more pleased with paintings representing things at home than sketches foreign to the state."

After much deliberation, the Commission reluctantly yielded to a legislative mandate and selected three of the state's leading painters— DeCamp, Edgar S. Paxson of Missoula, and Charles M. Russell, "the Cowboy Artist," from Great Falls. Butte's Hennessy Mercantile Company was chosen to coordinate the overall decoration of the new wings—a task that F. Pedretti's Sons had earlier combined with mural painting—to ensure that the efforts of the three Montana artists and others involved in outfitting the wings would result in "a harmonious whole."

In addition to the new construction, the expansion project also entailed remodeling portions of the original building and relocating various offices and functions. Most notably, the House moved into new quarters in the west wing; the Senate moved across the Rotunda into the former House; and the Supreme Court occupied the chamber on the east side of the Rotunda vacated by the Senate. A new Law Library and suite of offices for the governor, including a formal reception room, were among the touted features of the east wing. With the ex-

ception of the Governor's Reception Room— which was decidedly English Tudor in appearance—the decorative scheme throughout the additions was designed to blend with the French Renaissance motif of the original building.

Although the new wings were no less enthusiastically received by the citizens of the Treasure State, their completion did not meet with the same fanfare that had marked the earlier milestones of the building's construction. With comparatively little ceremony, the new wings were showcased during an open house held in conjunction with the State Fair. On the evening of September 27, 1912, members of the Board of Examiners and other state officers greeted visitors who had come to tour the renovation. Most exciting to all were the murals created by the trio of Montana artists. Acting on behalf of the Treasure State's citizenry, in 1913 the legislature passed a joint resolution thanking the three men for their work and presciently declaring that the "three notable artists of our state . . . have adorned these walls with masterpieces, that will be enduring monuments to themselves, and a lasting source of pride for the people of this commonwealth."

WITH THE COMPLETION of the wings, Montana's statehouse assumed its present-day exterior configuration. Since 1912, additional space for state government has been secured by constructing separate buildings, primarily in the vicinity of the Capitol, rather than by adding to the statehouse itself. Anyone familiar with the Capitol in 1912, therefore, could easily recognize the building today. Of course, minor changes have occurred—the original windows have been replaced, the north stairs have been altered to accommodate a drive-through, preservation measures have been implemented, and the landscaping has matured—but, overall, the Capitol remains the same building prized by earlier generations of Montanans.

Due to the demands of use and the changing dictates of style, however, the building's interior

Truly the "people's house," the Capitol has served as the setting for such diverse activities as political rallies and demonstrations, memorial observances, and public celebrations. Above, Helena High School students celebrate May Day in 1916; below, the Montana Highway Patrol shows off its new fleet in 1935.

A Civil Works Administration crew pauses from its task of applying new copper sheeting to the Capitol Dome in 1934. The Anaconda Company donated the copper after the public protested an unfortunate decision to paint the dome with aluminum paint.

has experienced a far greater number of changes than its exterior. During the 1930s, Works Progress Administration workers painted the walls of the Rotunda and the adjacent galleries, covering the original Pedretti decorations with a less colorful faux ashlar design. Driven by the critical need for structural reinforcement to decrease the potential for earthquake damage, extensive renovation efforts were undertaken in the 1950s and continued into the 1960s.

This structural safeguarding was accompanied by changes—aimed at modernizing the building—that dramatically altered many of the features that had characterized the Capitol's interior. Most significant were the removal of the art glass barrel vault that had crowned the Grand Stairway; the replacement of the glass-block Rotunda floor with terrazzo; extensive remodeling of the Senate Chamber; and cosmetic alterations designed to bring the sixty-year-old decor in line with contemporary tastes. In 1982, when the new Justice Building was constructed, the Law Library was moved out of the Capitol, and the former showplace was unceremoniously transformed into a legislative hearing room. Fortunately, in spite of the many changes that did occur, the importance of the thirty-five murals that adorn the statehouse was always fully realized, and no serious effort was ever undertaken to alter these colorful tributes to Montana's past.

By the closing decades of the twentieth century, Montana's Capitol was once again in need of attention. As with the renovation efforts of the 1950s and 1960s, the aging building required both structural repair and operational updating. This time, however, there was one major difference. Rather than attempting to make the statehouse look modern, the project sought to restore the building's interior to its original appearance. Wherever feasible, planners worked to return the Capitol to its former grandeur while ensuring that it continued to meet the demands of an ever-changing technological society. From the return of the art glass barrel

While renovation work in the 1950s and 1960s centered on earthquake-proofing and modernization, it also entailed the removal of much of the historic fabric of the building's interior.

In 1928, the Montana Historical Society's display cases boasted a wide variety of natural history specimens, historical artifacts, and curios. The Society was housed on the Capitol's first floor from 1902 until 1952, when it moved across the street to new headquarters in the Montana Veterans and Pioneers Memorial Building.

vault and reproduction of the original Pedretti paint schemes for the walls of the Rotunda, to the installation of replica doorknobs bearing the State Seal, every reasonable effort was made to restore the original vision of the building's designers. Installation of air conditioning and wiring for laptop computers went hand in hand with the return of original and reproduction chandeliers and the laying of ornate ceramic tile floors. The result is a statehouse functionally equipped for the twenty-first century, but one that would—as our forebears intended—continue to fulfill majestically its role as a "temple of democracy," a true house for the people.

PHOTOGRAPH BY GEORGE LANE/*INDEPENDENT RECORD*

PHOTOGRAPH BY TOM FERRIS

After the barrel vault was removed in 1964 to make room for a fourth-floor hearing room, it was replaced with a false skylight (see photograph above). Highlights of the 1999–2000 restoration included the return of the art glass barrel vault (shown in the photograph below under construction) and the original Pedretti decorative paint schemes to the Rotunda. The Pedrettis' decorations (partially uncovered below, left) had been painted over with the faux ashlar design in 1936.

PHOTOGRAPH BY J. M. COOPER

The Rotunda, showpiece of Montana's statehouse, photographed shortly after the building's completion (left) and after the 1999–2000 restoration (below).

29

The ART

PHOTOGRAPH BY TOM FERRIS

THE
PAINTINGS

PATRICIA M. BURNHAM*

*I wish to thank the following people: the staff at the Montana Historical Society, especially library, curatorial, education, and photo archives personnel, and, most especially, research historian Dave Walter; Marilyn Clifton Davis, Ohio Statehouse and Visitors Center, for information regarding the Pedretti family; Alfred C. Harrison, Jr., president of the North Point Gallery in San Francisco; and Arthur Lawrence, librarian and archivist, Union League Club of New York, for information about Amédée Joullin; and John Koerth of Helena, for information about mining in Montana. I am also indebted to the following institutions for funding: the Montana Historical Society, Senior Bradley Fellowship (1997); National Endowment for the Humanities, Summer Stipend (1994); and The University of Texas at Austin, College of Fine Arts, Faculty Travel Grants (1998–2001).

DECORATING THE CAPITOL

THE MONTANA CAPITOL art program produced one of the richest troves of statehouse art in the country: thirty-one paintings completed by an architectural decorating firm and four individual artists over a ten-year period in the early twentieth century, with four more paintings added in the late 1920s. Its significance, however, lies not in the number of paintings but in their cumulative effect: the stories that they tell, their aesthetic appeal, and their relationship to the building that houses them. This effect is not happenstance. It is the result of a series of choices made by the original Capitol Commission in 1902 and its successor in 1911.

Just as did other states in the Union, Montana wanted the art in its statehouse to be more than pretty pictures. The painted stories that would line the walls of the Capitol needed to convey both the essence of the state's history and the significance of its government. By tradition, these paintings needed to be a specific kind of art—mural art—large paintings either painted directly on the wall or on canvases that were affixed to the wall. Unlike portable easel paintings, murals are designed for specific locales, and their messages stay with the building to which the paintings are joined. Serious in content and elevated in tone, such art was meant to impress the public with the importance, dignity, and virtue of governmental activity. Thus, choosing the Capitol's art was an important cultural task.

The choices made by the commissions entrusted with the task of selecting the Capitol art must be understood in the context of the times. Building and decorating the Capitol coincided with a pivotal moment in American cultural history called the American Renaissance. Although it took its inspiration from classical forms, its energy from the Italian Renaissance, and its building principles from the Ecole des Beaux-Arts in France, the movement eloquently expressed American geopolitical aims. Poised

Centrally placed and hierarchically positioned, the Grand Stairway is the repository of the greatest amount of concentrated decoration in all the Capitol.

at the beginning of the new century, the confident, growing, and increasingly prosperous United States found the new neoclassicism of the American Renaissance consonant with its new status. The famous "White City" of the 1893 World's Columbian Exposition in Chicago quickly became the American Renaissance's leading exemplar, influencing an entire generation of public buildings. In particular, the many state capitols either newly built or rebuilt during the next two decades followed its lead in architectural style and mode of interior decoration.

American Renaissance mural painting leaned toward a more intellectual art, one that required thought, contemplation, and an appreciation of classical culture. Its artists were fine draftsmen who had trained in France and who worked closely with architects in creating a unified ensemble of art and architecture—one of the most important legacies of the Columbian Exposition. The themes were universal—Justice, Plenty, Peace—and the presentation allegorical. When the State of Minnesota, for example, wanted an image expressive of its agricultural wealth for its state capitol, it commissioned a French-trained artist from the Northeast to paint the allegory *Minnesota, Granary of the World*. The painting featured a female personification in classical garb surrounded by symbols of abundance that seemed at one with the setting for which it was made.

A challenge to the ascendancy of allegorical art came at the turn of the century from United States–trained illustrators. These artists argued that, instead of creating allegories that required a classical education to understand, public art should tell stories of real people and real events in a vernacular style. In this view, storytelling art was more accessible and, therefore, ultimately more democratic. Besides, it cost less than the allegorical art created by French-trained artists, and members of the general public liked it better. As a rule, however, architects and cosmopolitan sophisticates generally preferred allegorical painters. Although the American illustrators were typically highly skilled draftsmen, they lacked the refinement and polish of their French-trained confreres and, to architects' dismay, proved less sensitive to the relationship between their paintings and the built environment they adorned.

While a national debate raged over what seemed to be two diametrically opposed approaches toward public art, Montana's Capitol Commission, charged with overseeing the first phase of interior decoration (1901–3), chose a compromise course. After announcing a nationwide competition and reviewing bids, they hired an architectural decorating firm from Cincinnati, F. Pedretti's Sons, to decorate the Capitol. F. Pedretti's Sons employed neither French-trained "fine" artists nor American illustrators. It was, instead, a firm of decorators with a solid European art education. Its principals, Charles and Raphael Pedretti, had a solid foundation in figure painting, and they knew how to get along with architects and integrate art appropriately into an architectural setting.

Although their choice of the Pedrettis showed a recognition that the paintings should complement the architecture, the Capitol Commission, led by Governor Joseph K. Toole, did not want allegorical paintings adorning the Capitol's walls. Instead, they asked the Pedrettis to paint scenes from Montana history. As Commission member A. D. Peck stated in his "Report of the Commission," delivered at the dedication in 1902, the paintings by F. Pedretti's Sons "were made with a view to being historical and commemorative rather than symbolical or allegorical. It was thought more fitting that the pioneers of Montana in religious and industrial lines should be accorded places of honor in her halls, than that those places should be filled with mythological gods even though representative of the best virtues and highest attainments."

The Pedrettis painted four roundels for the Rotunda, six murals for the House of Representatives (now the Senate Chamber), and seven for the Senate (now the Old Supreme Court Chamber Hearing Room), but covering large areas of public space with figure paintings was only part of their mandate. Their job as decorators also involved stenciling walls and ceilings and making an art glass window for the head of the Grand Stairway. Even the paintings themselves were to be further embellished—that is, set into decorative spaces with gilded borders surrounded by stenciled designs.

The governor and his committee thus succeeded in their quest to make sure that the artwork would look professionally painted, that viewers could "read" stories from Montana life, and, above all, that the standards of decoration would be met—all at a cost the cramped state budget could bear. Sacrificed, perhaps, was historical accuracy and imagination in some of the Pedretti paintings, for the Pedrettis were not, in fact, trained history painters—a signal weakness they brought to the commission. To compensate, Governor Toole himself took on, with mixed results, the responsibility of choosing the scenes they were to portray and guiding their interpretation.

Montana did obtain the services of a French-trained artist at the end of the day, albeit under unusual circumstances. For the most prominent site in the Capitol, the area just above the art

F. Pedretti's Sons. Ornamentation, 1902.
Rotunda

F. Pedretti's Sons. Ornamentation, 1902. East Gallery

Much of the Capitol's overall aesthetic appeal comes from
F. Pedretti's Sons simulated sculptural reliefs, metal ornaments,
and stenciled borders, such as those detailed here.

glass window at the top of the Grand Stairway, Governor Toole originally had asked the Pedrettis for a painting celebrating a triumphant moment in the state's history—the completion of a transcontinental railway at Gold Creek, Montana. Before the Pedrettis could carry out the commission, however, the Northern Pacific Railroad offered to finance and commission the painting itself. Governor Toole found the deal eminently satisfactory. In this manner, California-born, French-trained Amédée Joullin came to paint *Driving the Golden Spike* in 1903, thus completing the first phase of Capitol decoration. It is the only one of the thirty-five Capitol murals not financed by public funds.

In 1909, the legislature—cramped for space—approved the addition of two wings onto the original building. This expansion occasioned a new opportunity for art to flourish at the Capitol. This time the choices made were dramatically different. Governor Edwin L. Norris and his committee, originally committed to the notion of commissioning nothing less than renowned French-trained artists from the Northeast, were trumped by legislative action. In February 1911, by joint resolution, the legislature stipulated that the Capitol imagery be based on "early Montana scenes and figures . . . and that such decorations be executed by Montana Artists of recognized ability and standing."

It is not clear if the legislators simply abhorred the thought of "aristocratic" artists being imported from the Northeast, found the Pedretti approach unsatisfactory, or were just flexing their populist muscles. At any rate, after a rigorous application process, three Montana artists were chosen: Edgar S. Paxson, Charles M. Russell, and Ralph E. DeCamp. In truth, there were few local artists other than these three who met the criteria of "recognized ability and standing." The governor and his Commission expressed strong reservations about these artists' competence, nevertheless.

In acquiescing to legislative action, the Capitol Commission had to give up all hope of allegories on the walls of the Capitol extension, but they did hold out for faithful artist cooperation with the architects to achieve a harmonious, decorative effect. The most coveted commission, a mural for the new House Chamber, went to Russell. Paxson was asked to paint six scenes for the House Lobby. DeCamp ultimately painted ten landscapes for the Law Library (now a series of hearing rooms), six during the art campaign of 1911–12 and four more in 1927–28. As for the decorative element, DeCamp did not need to strive after decorative effect since his lyrical landscapes performed that function so naturally. The records show and the paintings indicate that Paxson made a conscientious effort to keep in mind the overall decorative scheme. On the contrary, Russell's *Lewis and Clark Meeting Indians at Ross' Hole* dominates the entire room by means of its size, epic scale, and rhetorical power, rendering the much vaunted goal of artist/architect collaboration void in his case.

PAINTING THE HISTORY

Despite its decorative function, narrative Capitol art is ultimately more about history than decoration. At the turn of the century, Montanans regarded it as a cultural imperative to retrace the steps of their comparatively short history in visual form in order to explain to themselves and to the nation how they had arrived at their present position. Two governors and their respective Capitol Commissions, the artists they employed, and such other leading citizens as they consulted were to varying degrees responsible for the historical interpretation that resulted.

Writing Montana's story meant making crucial decisions about what to include and, as significantly, what to leave out. Studiously avoided were scenes of acerbic labor disputes, mining accidents, and political corruption—all important, if inglorious aspects of Montana's history. Rather, to fulfill the function of public art—in this case the celebration of a people's progress—the State, as governments routinely do, cleaned up the past for public consumption.

The topic occurring most often in the Capitol paintings is relations between Indians and Euro-Americans. Excluding the ten DeCamp landscapes, eleven of the twenty-five narrative paintings touch on Indian-white relations directly, and Native Americans appear in three more. Two of the DeCamp landscapes also allude to Indian culture. Clearly, Montana was preoccupied with the theme, measuring its progress by the distance it established from Indian culture with astonishing frankness. Admiring, polite, condescending, and angry in turn, the overriding attitude was one of presumed superiority of Euro-American culture.

The pride of place on the Capitol walls was given over to the icon of progress, the railroad. By installing Joullin's *Driving the Golden Spike* at the very head of the Grand Stairway, state leaders emphasized the arrival of the railroad in Montana over other aspects of state history. They did so because they thought that, more than any other factor, it incorporated Montana into the United States.

These choices reflected the Capitol Commission's understanding of history. The paintings on the Capitol walls are more than a mere chronological narrative of Montana events. Rather, the depicted episodes were chosen to reward pictorially progress and virtue. Overpowering the Indian by cultural as well as military means was a sign of progress. Major technological advances such as the railroad certainly brought progress. Emphatically, so did statehood. Military men such as General Nelson A. Miles made good heroes—although so did Chief Joseph and Chief Charlo. George Armstrong Custer, of course, was the preeminent military hero. In Paxson's eyes, Sacagawea was also heroic. Their choice of heroes and uncritical devotion to the concept of progress mark the artists and members of the Capitol Commission as children of the Progressive Era.

Today's viewers especially notice the gender bias of the era's historical vision. The story told in the Capitol art is one of male conquest. While a few white women are shown cowering inside Conestoga wagons and some native women fill in the background of the Russell picture, the world portrayed is a man's world. Sacagawea, an Indian interpreter with the Lewis and Clark

F. Pedretti's Sons. *Lewis' First Glimpse of the Rockies*, 1902. Oil on canvas, 84"×132". Old Supreme Court Chamber

So important did the Lewis and Clark Expedition seem to turn-of-the-century Montanans that all of the Capitol artists except Joullin painted the subject. In this painting, F. Pedretti's Sons depict Meriwether Lewis viewing for the first time the formidable mountain ranges that lay between the Corps of Discovery and the Pacific Ocean. Using an unusual visual strategy, the Pedretti artist invites the viewer to experience the moment through the act of Lewis's observation rather than focusing on what he actually saw.

Expedition, makes several grand appearances. (Paxson's valorization of her probably reflects her adoption by the women's suffrage movement as one of their foremothers.) Nevertheless, it is men who explore, trade, mine, make war, and tend to governmental affairs on the walls of the Capitol.

How would turn-of-the century viewers have judged the success or failure of the Capitol's history paintings? The answer seems to be by the murals' accuracy: accuracy in who is portrayed as present at historical events and in the flora and fauna of specific locales; accuracy in the likenesses of historical personages and correct costuming of Indians. This overarching concern for factual accuracy masked the larger question:

whose history is it, anyhow? Is it not also the history of those left off the walls, that of women as well as men, of losers as well as winners, of the Chinese who helped build the railroad as well as the rich investors who attended the Last Spike ceremony?

Twenty-first-century perspectives bring these questions to the fore. But even as we exercise our critical faculties as a veritable civic duty, it behooves us to view the Capitol art as an artifact of its time and to acknowledge the achievement of those who worked to make the Capitol an oasis of beauty and a citadel of meaning. F. Pedretti's Sons succeeded in creating a full-scale visual environment that was aesthetically pleasing,

Ralph E. DeCamp. *The Bitter Root*, 1911. Oil on canvas, 42"×83". Old Law Library

harmonious, and modern-looking to turn-of-the-century eyes. Notwithstanding their limitations as artists and historians, the Pedrettis conferred a sense of cultural respectability that the new state thought it needed. Joullin, who painted *Driving the Golden Spike*, showed himself to be eminently capable of producing a public-occasion piece on a large scale, an achievement that earned him many accolades when it was first exhibited.

As for the dismissive view that illustrators such as Russell and Paxson were mere storytellers, the criticism can be turned on its head. Their gift for creating deeply realized visual narratives has stimulated the minds and moved the hearts of thousands of viewers over the years. They were the best historians of the lot, men who at least tried to grapple with the issues of frontier history. Finally, DeCamp's luminous canvases, beaming down beautifully rendered images of Montana scenery, bestow a true spirit of peace and reconciliation between nature and society on all who view them.

The Pedrettis

A FOLLOWER OF Italian patriot Guiseppe Garibaldi, Francis Pedretti (1829-1891) fled Italy in the wake of the failed Revolution of 1848 for New York City, where the young artist began a career as a fresco painter. Trained at the Brera Academy of Fine Arts in Milan, he brought with him a tradition of European craftsmanship and familiarity with the requirements of mural art. Because such skills were in relatively short supply in the United States, he quickly found a niche for himself as an architectural decorator. Hired by architect Isaiah Rogers to decorate the Astor Hotel in New York, he followed Rogers to Cincinnati, Ohio. There he opened his own firm, which became a leading establishment of its kind, its reputation extending well beyond city and even state limits.

In 1887, Francis Pedretti formed a partnership with his sons, Raphael M. Pedretti (1858–1929) and Charles A. Pedretti (1864–1941), which eventually took the name of F. Pedretti's Sons. Both sons, also trained in Italy, continued the successful professional practice of their father into the twentieth century. Together, Raphael and Charles Pedretti decorated hotels, churches, synagogues, and other public and private buildings until their partnership dissolved in 1905. Perhaps their most notable commission in Ohio, undertaken just before the Montana project, was the four allegorical panels they painted for the Capitol Annex in Columbus.

Of the two brothers, Charles was the one more involved in the decoration of the Montana Capitol. According to E. B. Kennedy, secretary of the Capitol Commission, "[t]he work was executed under [his] personal supervision . . . [and he] prepared all the designs, selected the colors and did much of the work himself." Although the brothers were trained fresco painters (that is, knew how to paint directly on the wet plaster of the wall itself), the Montana murals were painted in oil on canvas in Ohio, shipped to Helena, then mounted on the walls of the Capitol. To install the paintings and complete the Capitol decoration, Pedretti brought experienced workmen with him from Ohio. Local newspapers followed the comings and goings with considerable interest. The Helena *Independent* announced on January 14, 1902, that Charles Pedretti had come to town "accompanied by Mrs. Pedretti" and seven workmen.

Governor Joseph K. Toole played an unusually active role in the first phase of Capitol decoration. Not only did he dictate the subjects for the Pedretti paintings, but he stipulated what form the paintings should take and often suggested specific visual sources from which the artists should work. In the interest of accuracy, Toole, or a member of the Commission, mailed photographs of historical personages to Cincinnati or informed the Pedrettis

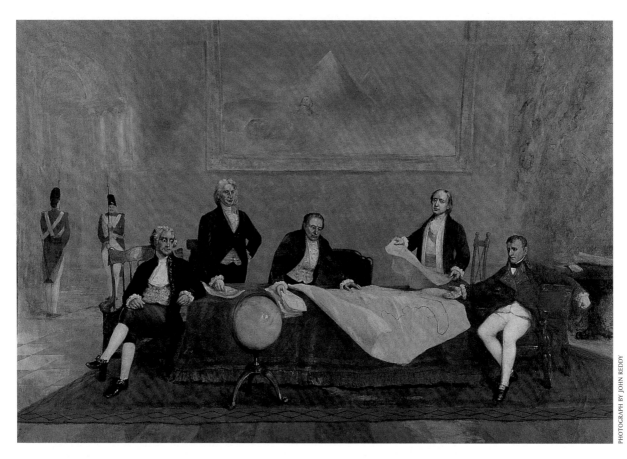

F. Pedretti's Sons. *The Louisiana Purchase,* 1902. Oil on canvas, 168"×204". Senate Chamber

This prominently placed mural honors the 1803 Louisiana Purchase, which made possible American settlement of the West. Depicted are the two heads of state, Napoléon and President Thomas Jefferson (who never actually met), the Marquis de Barbé-Marbois, Robert Livingston, and future president James Monroe, who conducted the negotiations. Behind the men is an image of the Sphinx and Egyptian pyramids—possibly an allusion to Napoléon's Egyptian campaign but more likely a reference to Masonic iconography. One of the weakest of the Pedretti firm's efforts technically, the painting nevertheless expresses Montanans' intense desire to historicize their experience and the significance they imputed to governmental arrangements.

where images might be found. Such support was typical for projects of this nature. More curious is Toole's intervention into what might have been considered the artists' essential creative process. For example, for *Lewis' First Glimpse of the Rockies,* Toole insisted that the Pedrettis use an illustration from *Scribner's Magazine* as the basis for the composition, which they indeed did. Nothing in the available record indicates that the Pedretti firm bridled at this intrusiveness, however.

Departures from fact abound in the Pedretti murals. One of the most blatant examples is the absurdly inappropriate clothing, pose, and lodging of Sacagawea in *Lewis and Clark at Three Forks* in the original House of Representatives. Because the Pedrettis were primarily decorators and not history painters, one is tempted to think of Toole himself as the errant historian. Given what we know about his intelligence, deep knowledge of Montana history, and commitment to historical accuracy, however, it is more probable that the hurried process interfered with conscientious supervision on his part. Or per-

F. Pedretti's Sons. *Custer's Last Battle*, 1902. Oil on canvas, 168"×204". Senate Chamber

Strategically placed opposite *The Louisiana Purchase* hangs *Custer's Last Battle,* which commemorates the death of George Armstrong Custer and the other army casualties at the Battle of Little Bighorn in eastern Montana on June 25, 1876. The charged space between the two paintings suggests the violent history that took place between 1803 and 1876. Because of the special demands of public decorative art (few figures, figure size consonant with other murals, limited violence), the Pedretti artists reduced the battle scene to a stark confrontation between Custer and an unidentified Sioux warrior.

haps the Pedrettis made up their own history and the errors were discovered too late?

The greatest achievement of the Pedrettis in the new Capitol was the decoration of the entire building, seen most spectacularly in the art glass window at the head of the Grand Stairway. The seventeen paintings shared in the decorative effect of the overall project. Each individual painting is carefully fitted into its space and coordinated thematically and aesthetically with its neighbor. Gilt borders and patterned stenciling act as complements to the paintings, thus integrating them into the room in which they hang. As visitors stroll through the Capitol today, they are more likely to laud the aesthetic experience of the whole than to deplore inaccuracies in historical details. At the 1902 dedication, E. B. Kennedy stated, "The harmony of the color effects . . . is wonderful, and the building has been given by [the Pedrettis] a character and beauty not surpassed by any building in the land." Although Kennedy may have exaggerated, his comments make clear the expectations of the time and the ability of the Pedrettis to meet them.

F. Pedretti's Sons. *The Trapper*, 1902. Oil on canvas, 84" in diameter. Rotunda

In the Rotunda, four large roundels summarize specific aspects of Montana history through paintings of real people, each of whom represents a general type. This roundel's image of famous mountain man Jim Bridger (1804–1881) acknowledges the contributions of trappers and explorers, who first opened up the mountain West for Euro-Americans.

F. Pedretti's Sons. *The Indian Chief,* 1902. Oil on canvas, 84" in diameter. Rotunda

Chosen to represent the pre-encounter history of the state is Salish chief Charlo (1830–1910), whose staunch resistance to the removal of his people from the Bitterroot Valley and eventual capitulation were still vivid memories in 1902. The choice of Charlo poses the interesting question as to whether Governor Toole (who selected the subject) wished to heroize Charlo for his resistance or his acquiescence.

F. Pedretti's Sons. *The Prospector,* 1902. Oil on canvas, 84" in diameter. Rotunda

The exploitation of Montana's vast mineral wealth originated with the humble efforts of prospectors such as Henry Finnis Edgar (1826–1910), pictured here with pickax and gold pan. Of the six men who discovered gold in Alder Gulch in 1863, Edgar achieved the greatest success and standing in the community. Perhaps Governor Toole thought that Edgar's reputation would give a patina of respectability to some of the rough edges of Montana's mining past.

F. Pedretti's Sons. *The Cowboy*, 1902. Oil on canvas, 84" in diameter. Rotunda

The cowboy, already a mythic figure by 1902, finds a place in the Rotunda not because of the romantic aura of his work but as a representative of the prosperity brought to Montana by the cattle industry. Curiously, this is the only one of the four roundels for which Governor Toole did not provide the name of a particular individual. For guidance, he instead referred the Pedretti firm to the paintings of Charles M. Russell.

F. Pedretti's Sons. *Old Fort Benton (Pierre Chouteau and Andrew Dawson)*, 1902. Oil on canvas, 168"×102". Senate Chamber

Old Fort Benton extends the theme of the fur trade beyond the trapper era celebrated in the Rotunda to the complex, expansive business it became in its later phase. Pictured are two well-known associates of the American Fur Company, which founded Fort Benton. Seated is Pierre Chouteau, Jr. (1789–1865), grandson of the founder of the city of St. Louis and scion of his family's fur business. Scottish-born Andrew Dawson (1817–1871), standing, ran Fort Benton between 1854 and 1865. Shown as a sprawling group of adobe brick buildings visible in the upper right side of the picture, Fort Benton was one of Montana's principal trading centers until the construction of the railroads. Tepees brushed in lightly reference the fort's original purpose—to expand market possibilities among the Blackfeet Indians.

F. Pedretti's Sons. *Old Fort Owen (Fathers Ravalli and DeSmet)*, 1902. Oil on canvas, 168"×102". Senate Chamber

Old Fort Owen, the titular subject, is relegated to the distant background; instead, two Jesuit priests, Anthony Ravalli, S.J. (1812–1884) and Pierre-Jean De Smet, S.J. (1801–1873), dominate the image. (The Salish child tucked under Ravalli's arm is shown in a pose borrowed from depictions of the infant Christ in Italian Renaissance painting, a cosmopolitanizing Pedretti touch.) A legendary figure in Montana history, Belgian-born De Smet established St. Mary's Mission in the Bitterroot Valley in 1841 in response to requests from several Indian delegations; Italian-born Ravalli followed five years later. When the mission closed in 1850, Major John Owen (1818–1889) purchased the building and developed the popular trading post that bore his name.

F. Pedretti's Sons. *Prospectors at Nelson Gulch*, 1902. Oil on canvas, 168"×102". Senate Chamber

Prospectors at Nelson Gulch depicts four men performing various tasks connected with placer mining, the original and most primitive phase of mining in Montana. The figure at right leaning over the pan is Jerry Robinson, while the man seated on the sluice is Isaac "Ike" Newcomer, two well-known old-timers who came to Montana in the 1860s. Although not one of the most famous mining sites, Nelson Gulch, located outside of Helena, enjoyed a high degree of productivity. Historicizing in intent, the scene is also romantic and nostalgic, far removed from the heavily industrialized mining of 1902.

F. Pedretti's Sons. *Gates of the Mountains*, 1902. Oil on canvas, 84"×120". Old Supreme Court Chamber

On July 19, 1805, journeying up the Missouri River from the Great Falls to the headwaters at the Three Forks, Meriwether Lewis and his men passed through a spot where the river narrows alarmingly, slicing the land into high cliffs on either side. Lewis named it the Gates of the Mountains, a geographical designation that is still used. The decision to depict a historic landscape rather than a peopled event (the only one among the seventeen paintings by F. Pedretti's Sons) was Governor Toole's. In terms of pure painting, it is the most satisfying of all the Pedretti paintings.

F. Pedretti's Sons. *Lewis and Clark at Three Forks*, 1902. Oil on canvas, 168"×102". Senate Chamber

In July 1805, Meriwether Lewis (1774–1809) and William Clark (1770–1838) reached a juncture critical to their journey: the Three Forks in southwest Montana that make up the Missouri River. Pictured are Lewis (standing) and Clark (seated), Lewis's slave York, and Indian interpreter Sacagawea. The scene looks more like a vacation picnic by the river than a moment resonant with historical meaning. The Pedretti formula of silhouetting visually convincing portraits against a realistic looking background that worked so well in paintings such as *Old Fort Benton* failed them on this occasion.

F. Pedretti's Sons. *Emigrant Train Being Attacked by the Indians*, 1902. Oil on canvas, 84"×132". Old Supreme Court Chamber

Although native attacks on emigrants did occur in Montana, they do not constitute a major aspect of state history. Did white fear of such an occurrence make it seem a more defining event in their history than the actual number of incidents would suggest? In appropriating this element of the classic western saga for Montanans, perhaps Governor Toole also thought to honor families as well as mountain men and prospectors as part of the heroic era of Montana's past.

FACING PAGE: F. Pedretti's Sons. *The Chase of the Buffalo,* 84"×132", and *Farewell to the Buffalo,* 84"×120", 1902. Oil on canvas. Old Supreme Court Chamber

Paired in meaning, these two murals portray the life and death of Plains Indian culture as it was understood at the beginning of the twentieth century. The chase scene, long a favorite of western artists, signified the buffalo economy of Montana natives. Over the corpse of the last buffalo, Indians weep and pray for the replenishment of the herd as a railroad train comes roaring into the picture space at the right. The railroad was not the innocuous agent of neutral progress, however, but a collusive factor in bringing about the very tragedy depicted in the painting. The death of the buffalo was generally understood to be a metaphor for the demise of Indian culture, which was thought to be imminent—but which did not happen.

F. Pedretti's Sons. *Signing of the Enabling Act* and *Signing the Proclamation of Statehood,* 1902. Oil on canvas, 84"×48". Old Supreme Court Chamber

The two statehood pictures valorize government procedures, acknowledge the triumph of law over frontier conditions, and celebrate the coming of age of Montana after a long and painful struggle. The signing of the Enabling Act on February 22, 1889, "enabled" Montana to become a state once the requirements for a state constitution were satisfied. In the picture, Secretary of State Thomas F. Bayard hands the bill to outgoing president Grover Cleveland as Joseph K. Toole, in his role of territorial delegate, looks on. Those requirements having been met, the second picture shows President Benjamin Harrison signing the proclamation declaring Montana a state on November 8, 1889, in the presence of Secretary of State James G. Blaine.

Amédée Joullin (1862–1917)

MUCH AMBIGUITY surrounds the commissioning of Amédée Joullin by the Northern Pacific Railroad to paint the most visible, most prominently placed work in the Capitol art program, *Driving the Golden Spike.* The son of French-born parents, Joullin was born in California, studied at the California School of Design in San Francisco (now the San Francisco Art Institute), and taught there from 1887 to 1897. A west coast critic described him in 1899 as "one of the better known of California artists . . . [who] wrested respectful and appreciative attention from the general and the critical public." For two years in the early 1880s, Joullin studied at the Ecole des Beaux-Arts and the Académie Julian in Paris with such luminaries as William-Adolphe Bouguereau, Jules Lefèbvre, and Robert Fleury, thereby establishing his credentials as a "modern" French-trained artist. After his return to California, he pioneered what were called "Chinatown genre" scenes, continued to produce California landscapes, and eventually branched off into Indian subjects, particularly Indians of the Southwest. Nowhere does the record indicate expertise on his part with mural art or the decoration of public buildings.

Nevertheless, Joullin was the Northern Pacific Railroad's pick for the commission. The nexus connecting him with the railroad, Governor Toole, and the State of Montana is still unknown. We know that Toole originally asked the Pedrettis to paint the Last Spike subject, that a subsidy offer came from the Northern Pacific (but the correspondence and connecting points are missing), and that the railroad's choice of artist was Joullin. We also know that the prestigious Union League Club of New York mounted a highly acclaimed exhibition of Joullin's paintings on western subjects in November 1901, which the California press suggested had brought him to the attention of art brokers for the Northern Pacific. By December 1901, the commission was his; as early as January the following year, Joullin was in Montana with his sleeves rolled up.

The subject of the painting and its location at the top of the Grand Stairway in the Capitol attest to the importance of the arrival of the railroad to Montanans. The first transcontinental railroad, the Union Pacific, which famously brought together the western and eastern halves of the nation at Promontory, Utah, in 1869, crossed Wyoming, not Montana. The clamor for a more northern transcontinental route was finally satisfied when the troubled Northern Pacific, under the new leadership of Henry Villard, not only traversed Montana but decided that its meeting point between east and west would be on Montana soil, close to Gold Creek (near present-day Drummond). A ceremony on September 8, 1883, which culminated the epic project, provided the moment depicted in the painting,

51

Amédée Joullin. *Driving the Golden Spike*, 1903. Oil on canvas, 183"×90". Grand Stairway

Driving the Golden Spike commemorates the completion of the transcontinental Northern Pacific Railroad on September 8, 1883, at Gold Creek, Montana, an important emblem of the state's modernization. Wielding the sledgehammer he will use to drive the spike stands former president Ulysses S. Grant. Smiling encouragingly, Northern Pacific president Henry Villard looks on from the right. The bearded gentleman behind Grant to the left is Secretary of the Interior Henry Moore Teller. Secretary of State William M. Evarts, principal orator at the event, stands just in front of Teller. At the lower left can be seen a delegation of Crow Indians, whose land the railroad crossed.

that of former president Ulysses S. Grant driving in the last spike as Northern Pacific president Villard looked on. Interestingly, at Villard's insistence, the spike used in the ceremony was not gold at all, but a working iron spike that reputedly had been used to initiate the transcontinental project in Minnesota in 1872. (This iron spike is in the collection of the Montana Historical Society; the location of the gold-plated spike produced for the occasion is unknown.)

Donning the mantle of history painter with great seriousness, Joullin conducted considerable historical research, much of it at the Montana Historical Society. He also made site sketches, and dependent on photographs as were all artists in similar circumstances, he built up a repertory of portrait shots of the prominent participants. He clearly based some of his artistic decisions on the availability of such photographic aids. For example, the delegation of

Crow Indians at the left, including Chief Iron Bull who was one of those designated to hammer the spike, is copied almost exactly from a photograph taken at the celebration by western photographer F. Jay Haynes. To people the background, Joullin tried to include generic types present at the event: soldiers, cowboys, miners, and railroad men. Nevertheless, the workers who physically built the railroad—the Irish, the Chinese, and others—are absent. In general, Joullin's approach is dignified and decorous in the manner of French-American official art. Sober colors dominate, except for the colorfully clad members of the Crow delegation, whom he painted in vivid hues and considerable detail.

First seen by the public in California and subsequently mounted in place at the Capitol, *Driving the Golden Spike* garnered high praise. Although today's viewers are painfully aware of the limitations of turn-of-the-century official commemorative art, the painting nevertheless summarizes the history of the railroad in a way that pleased its original audience: the company that paid the money, the governor who oversaw its creation, and the public for which it was intended.

Edgar Samuel Paxson (1852–1919)

Of the three Montana artists chosen to produce murals for the Capitol expansion in 1911, Edgar S. Paxson was arguably the most respected at the time. Twelve years older than Russell and without a wild past to overcome, Paxson had earned a measure of esteem in Montana. His professional standing was secured in 1899 when he completed his version of the Battle of Little Bighorn, *Custer's Last Stand* (now owned by the Whitney Gallery of Western Art, Buffalo Bill Historical Center). A large painting crammed full of visual information about the battle, it became the favorite of an entire generation of Montanans.

A person of humble origins and modest means, Paxson was born in 1852 near Buffalo, New York. His first experience in the arts was helping his father decorate carriages at a nearby factory. When he left New York for Montana in 1877, he already had assumed the responsibilities of marriage and fatherhood. His first year on the frontier was spent riding shotgun for Overland Stage Company and possibly working as an army scout. The following year found him in Deer Lodge, where he commenced a career in sign painting. After he and his family moved to Butte in 1880, he entered a second line of work, scene painting, which resulted in major commissions for the Renshaw Opera House and Maguire's Grand Opera House in Butte. At this point, he also began—without any substan-

tive training—to produce easel paintings of western subjects.

Paxson soon established a reputation for frontier scenes and Native American portraits. He exhibited at the World's Columbian Exposition in Chicago in 1893, at the Louisiana Purchase Exposition in St. Louis in 1904, and the Lewis and Clark Centennial Exposition in Portland in 1905. He finished his well-known *Custer's Last Stand* in 1899 to great acclaim. By 1901 the press was acclaiming his talent as a leading "Indian painter." After he moved to Missoula in 1906, he began to sell nationally and internationally and expanded his repertoire to include postcard and book illustrations. At no point did he ever achieve the status, make the income, or lead the glamorous life that Russell did in his later years, but he was greatly admired locally. His studio became a mecca for visitors—native and white—and his house a bastion of western hospitality. Paxson completed his second major mural commission in 1917 for the Missoula County Courthouse—eight paintings depicting scenes from western Montana history. He died in Missoula in 1919 at the age of sixty-seven.

The State of Montana commissioned six paintings for the Capitol from Paxson for the sum of fifteen hundred dollars. Whereas Governor Toole had chosen the subjects for the paintings created by F. Pedretti's Sons during the first phase of Capitol decoration, the Norris administration, which oversaw decoration of the addition, gave Paxson comparatively free rein. Paxson selected his own topics (subject to veto only), and the Capitol Commission refrained from telling him how to go about his business. His relationship with government officials had its own problems, however. Paxson complained about having to submit preliminary sketches for each of the six paintings and afterwards about the delay in returning the sketches to him. With more justification, he objected to consistent misspelling of his name—especially in his contract. One of the subjects he proposed was dismissed because the action took place in Idaho. Another was rejected because Russell had already chosen it—which aggravated Paxson greatly. The most serious problem that developed was that four of the six paintings turned out to be too small for the spaces for which they were intended. (This was probably not Paxson's fault, although the record is not completely clear on this point.) However, Paxson commenced and completed his paintings ahead of schedule, which endeared him to Governor Norris.

The breadth of Paxson's historical interests can be seen in the range of subjects he depicted. It was Paxson, after all, who pushed the Capitol's visual history of Montana back to its earliest conceivable European presence—French trader Pierre de La Vérendrye's forays into the Missouri River Valley in the 1740s. Paxson painted two requisite scenes from the Lewis and Clark journey, *Lewis at Black Eagle Falls* and *Lewis and Clark at Three Forks*, but neither is formulaic. Compared to the weak scene of the Three Forks incident by the Pedrettis, Paxson's version successfully communicates the significance of the occasion. *After the Whiteman's Book* portrays an important episode from post-encounter Salish history and *Surrender of Chief Joseph* the denouement of the tragic conflict between the army and the Nez Perce that took place on Montana soil. *The Border Land* shows representative natives and whites taking each other's measure across a stream that functions as a natural border—an ambitious attempt to transcend mere reportage of specific historical incidents in order to make a more generalized statement. It is obvious that Paxson understood Montana history in terms of native-white conflict and wanted his paintings to comment visually on that understanding. Although he personally admired Chief Joseph's integrity and the religious enthusiasm of the Salish delegation, he stopped short of supporting Indian rights in general.

In researching his topics, Paxson followed a path similar to Russell's. He made use of library facilities in Butte in his earlier years and subsequently in Missoula. Extended contact with Montana pioneer and historian Granville Stuart in Butte also gave him access to historical sources. Observers noted that he had practically memorized the *Journals of Lewis and Clark*. Paxson also showed great respect for oral tradition, especially that of native peoples. For example, to depict in *After the Whiteman's Book* the treks by combined parties of Salish, Nez Perce, and Iroquois to St. Louis in the 1830s, he apparently interviewed Salish leader Louison, whose uncle had accompanied the original delegation.

Strength of characterization and intensity of feeling distinguish Paxson's murals. His lack of training in drawing and anatomy occasionally undercuts his aesthetic achievement, but, in the end, it is his success in dramatizing that we remember—the intensity of the gaze on Chief Joseph's face as he gives his surrender speech (even though present-day scholars doubt that Joseph actually said the words attributed to him), the determination of the Salish pilgrimaging to St. Louis to find the powerful blackrobes'

FACING PAGE: A western artist's studio functioned not just as his workplace, but as the nerve center of his overall creative effort. Edgar S. Paxson is shown here in his Butte studio in the early 1900s, surrounded by his large collection of Indian and other artifacts.

Edgar S. Paxson. *After the Whiteman's Book,* 1912. Oil on canvas, 81"×47". House Lobby

Paxson professed himself very moved by the story of the Salish-led spiritual pilgrimage from the Bitterroot Valley to St. Louis to find powerful white medicine—the Bible of the "blackrobes," or Jesuits. Four groups of Indians attempted the trip during the 1830s before Pierre-Jean De Smet, S.J. (depicted elsewhere on the Capitol walls) answered their call in 1841. Presumably, this painting records the initial expedition of 1831. Against a background of the high Bitterroot Mountains, the determination of the group is emphasized in the strong stride and concentrated expression of the foreground figure.

Edgar S. Paxson. *The Border Land,* 1912. Oil on canvas, 81"×153". House Lobby

The only one of Paxson's six paintings lacking a reference to historic personages, *The Border Land* comments on Indian-white conflict using generic types. Running along a diagonal that begins at the lower left, a creek creates a natural barrier that is also symbolic of a border between peoples. Settlers (he expressly avoids using trappers, explorers, or miners) confront Indians who respond with an enigmatic gesture that may signify peace—or then again, halt.

book (the Bible of the Jesuit missionaries), Sacagawea's bold stance in pointing out the site of her abduction several years earlier to Lewis and Clark. Perhaps Paxson's experience in scene painting brought him closer to the invented worlds of the theater, which he then transferred to canvas.

Second only to the Pedrettis', Paxson's murals were also supremely decorative. The Capitol Commission lectured all three artists firmly on their responsibility to harmonize with the color scheme, but Paxson is the one who seems to have taken the advice most seriously. The larger paintings, *The Border Land* and *Lewis and Clark at Three Forks,* gave him ample opportunity to practice his skill in depicting "scenic" landscape backgrounds. It is his use of painted borders with decorative titles, however, which create an attractive transition from picture tones to wall tints, that qualifies him as a "decorator." Paxson is the only one of the Capitol artists to use this device, and it is not clear why he did so. Was it indeed a conscious response to the Commission's mandate? Might it

have been a practical solution to the problem of paintings too small for their spaces? Did he borrow it from the conventions of book illustration, with which he was so familiar? Or was it simply an aesthetic decision emerging from his work as sign painter? Whatever Paxson's motivation, the effect gave a look of finish and elegance to the House Lobby.

Although the House Lobby acts as an introductory area to the main chamber, visually as well as spatially, Paxson's paintings do not just lead to the Russell within but maintain a sense of their own individuality. Instead of the vast panoramic view seen from a distance that Russell offers in *Lewis and Clark Meeting Indians at Ross' Hole,* Paxson's paintings are at once closer to the picture plane and physically closer to the viewer, resulting in a heightened sense of immediacy. Taken together, the six paintings by Paxson in the House Lobby and the Russell painting in the House Chamber itself extend the range of subject matter in the Capitol in meaningful ways and probe historical events with psychological insight and historical understanding.

Edgar S. Paxson. *Lewis at Black Eagle Falls*, 1912. Oil on canvas, 81"×39". House Lobby

Meriwether Lewis's arrival at the series of five waterfalls in Cascade County on June 13–14, 1805, evoked some of the most effusive prose in all of his writings. Although he lavished his greatest praise on Great Falls and Rainbow Falls, he expressed tender regard for Black Eagle Falls because it boasted in its midst an island featuring a black eagle's nest atop a cottonwood tree. Perhaps this is why Paxson chose to depict Black Eagle Falls in this painting, which includes the island with a cottonwood tree (but, surprisingly, no eagle's nest). The standing figure on the left is Lewis; his companion in the picture cannot be identified because, in reality, Lewis undertook this particular exploration alone.

59

Edgar S. Paxson. *Pierre de La Vérendrye*, 1912. Oil on canvas, 81"×39". House Lobby

In this painting, Paxson depicts French-Canadian trader and explorer Pierre Gaultier de Varenne, Sieur de La Vérendrye (1685–1749), who at that time was believed to be the first white man to reach what is now Montana. More likely it was one of Vérendrye's sons who, in the company of an Indian war party on January 1, 1743, encountered mysterious "shining mountains," possibly in the region of the Bighorn Mountains. Whatever the facts of the matter, Paxson distinguishes himself as the only one of the Capitol artists to pay homage to the early French presence in the Northwest.

Edgar S. Paxson. *Lewis and Clark at Three Forks,* 1912. Oil on canvas, 81"×153". House Lobby

Two great moments converged for the Lewis and Clark Expedition in late July 1805: their arrival at the Three Forks that made up the headwaters of the Missouri River and Sacagawea's recognition of her people's hunting grounds from which she had been abducted five years earlier. The stream in the right mid-ground signifies the importance of the geographical discovery, and Sacagawea's bold signal, the encouraging probability that her people would soon be found. Sacagawea's pointing motion, although satisfying dramatically, was not a gesture that either the Hidatsa (her captors) or the Shoshone (her people) would have sanctioned. Clark (at left) and Lewis flank Sacagawea; to the right is her husband, fellow interpreter Toussaint Charbonneau. At the far left are explorer John Colter and the African American slave of Clark, known as York.

FACING PAGE: Edgar S. Paxson. *Surrender of Chief Joseph*, 1912. Oil on canvas, 81"×47". House Lobby

On October 5, 1877, Nez Perce leader Heinmot Tooyalakekt (1840–1904), popularly known as Chief Joseph, surrendered to the United States Army near the Bears Paw Mountains in northern Montana after a long, heroic struggle. Paxson captures the dramatic moment when Chief Joseph turned over his rifle and reportedly gave his famous speech, which closed with the ringing words, "From where the sun now stands I will fight no more forever." The artist expended every effort to ensure accuracy in presentation, from the gesture of Chief Joseph's upswept arm to the likenesses of the principal actors, Gen. Nelson A. Miles, Gen. Oliver O. Howard (in buckskin behind Miles), and Chief Joseph himself.

Charles Marion Russell (1864–1926)

NO ONE IN Montana in 1901 would have predicted that slightly more than a decade later a painting by Charlie Russell would be the pride of the state Capitol. Dedicated as they were to the notion of European-educated figure painters (even if only decorators), the Toole Capitol Commission saw no serious role for a western artist such as Russell in the first phase of the Capitol art program. The Commission made only minimal use of his talents—Toole recommended some of Russell's works as visual aids to the Pedrettis (particularly for *The Cowboy*) and used a design by Russell as the cover for the dedication program.

Two significant developments between the conclusion of the first phase of Capitol decoration in 1903 and preparations for the second phase in 1911 explain the difference in artistic climate. The populist explosion in the legislature demanding Montana subjects painted by Montana artists made local artists such as Russell eligible for consideration. Of equal importance, Russell's artistic reputation had grown dramatically in the eight-year interim.

The story of Russell's rise to prominence is one of the great sagas of American art history. Born into a family of good standing in St. Louis, Missouri, in 1864, Russell resisted formal schooling as much as possible and lit out for the wilds of Montana when he was only sixteen. He spent the next dozen years living hand to mouth, wrangling horses and pursuing related activities on the frontier, and fitting in art when and where he could. Russell traded in the cowboy life for that of full-time artist in 1893 and married and settled down in 1896. With the beginning of the new century, his career began to take off. Four of his paintings were exhibited at the 1904 Louisiana Purchase Exposition. People began to refer to him as the logical successor to Frederic Remington even before Remington's untimely death in 1909. A one-man exhibition at the prestigious Folsom Galleries in New York and the acceptance of one of his bronzes at the 1911 International Exposition in Rome gained him additional renown.

Impressing the cultural arbiters of the State of Montana remained an elusive goal, however. While the legislature wanted the Capitol decorated by Montana artists, the Capitol Commission continued to press for an experienced eastern muralist to create the large painting for the House. Even after choosing Russell for the job, members of the Capitol Commission continued to make their disappointment known. Furthermore, architect Frank Andrews, who lobbied for high-class decorative painter Gilbert White, expressed his anger at not being consulted during the decision-making process. Russell had his own supporters, however, among them Montana secretary of state A. N. Yoder and writer Frank Bird Linderman, who at this time was serving as Yoder's assistant secretary of state.

PHOTOGRAPH BY HEYNS ELITE STUDIO, GREAT FALLS

Charles M. Russell is pictured here in 1912 in his Great Falls studio working on *Lewis and Clark Meeting Indians at Ross' Hole*.

Amid the controversy Russell, Paxson, and DeCamp followed established procedures for applicants, coming to Helena for interviews with the Capitol Commission (Russell from Great Falls) and submitting formal sketches. In July 1911, the State of Montana contracted to render five thousand dollars to Charles M. Russell upon completion of a painting for the large wall behind the speaker's rostrum of the House of Representatives.

Controversy continued to cloud the proceedings, however. Russell's first two subjects for the proposed painting were rejected: Lewis's meeting with the Shoshones because it took place in Idaho and an Indian attack on a wagon train on the grounds that it "does not appeal to us as a suitable decoration for the House of Representatives." The meeting between Lewis and Clark and the Salish at Ross's Hole emerged as the most propitious topic only after extended colloquy among Russell, Governor Norris, and Judge William Y. Pemberton, a distinguished Montana jurist with a strong interest in Lewis and Clark. Then there was the matter of the size of the painting. The dimensions orally communicated to Russell and those written in the contract were different. Russell failed to question the discrepancy and bought expensive canvas according to the incorrect written instructions, which brought down on him the intemperate wrath of the Commission. Fortunately, the error was caught in time, and the Commission even reimbursed Russell for money spent on the wrong canvas.

The third and most serious conflict between Russell and the governor concerned timing. Norris visited Great Falls in April 1912 only to discover that Russell had not even commenced work on the mural. Heated exchanges filled the air for weeks to come. Russell turned up the pressure on himself, however, and delivered the finished painting ahead of schedule in July.

After overcoming some initial nervousness about his readiness to take on a job for which he was not adequately trained, Russell went about the task with dispatch. His first act was to raise the ceiling on his studio to accommodate the canvas's large size. He asked friends and associates near and far for their advice although in the end he went his own way. Like any history painter, he made careful preparatory drawings of some of the figures, working especially hard on the pose of the mounted warrior in the foreground. And he made a special sketching trip to the Bitterroot Valley to assure the accuracy of the mountain background. Acting as his own historian, he made astute use of historical materials in the Great Falls library and drew upon his personal collection of Indian artifacts (although not always correctly).

Lewis and Clark Meeting Indians at Ross' Hole celebrates the fortuitous encounter between the Corps of Discovery and the Salish people on September 4, 1805, which enabled the explorers to replenish essential horse stock and obtain directions for the final push over the Bitterroot Mountains to the Pacific. The moment was one of enormous strategic importance to the success of the trek. It also had excellent pictorial potential: beautiful scenery, "picturesque" Indians, and visually interesting rituals governing the meeting. Russell made the most of all these possibilities.

The final result is grander than could ever have been anticipated, perhaps even by Russell himself. *Lewis and Clark Meeting Indians at Ross' Hole* dominates its space not only physically, but psychologically and, perhaps one might say, even morally. By far the largest painting in the Capitol at twelve feet by twenty-four feet, it achieves superiority in sheer size even over Joullin's *Driving the Golden Spike*. Furthermore, the House Chamber is the only major decorated room in the Capitol with but a single space for art, so the painting has no visual competition. Far beyond what the architectural design contributed to the general effect, however, is what Russell himself accomplished in manipulating the interplay between real space and the simulated space within the picture. A more traditional approach might have foregrounded the principal actors in a static row parallel to the picture plane. Instead, with a sweep of horses, Salish warriors, and tilted lances in the center foreground, Russell

The new House of Representatives, part of the expansion completed in 1912, departed radically from its Pedretti-decorated predecessor. Its simple, sleeker look may well have seemed more "modern." A sole painting—Charles M. Russell's *Lewis and Clark Meeting Indians at Ross' Hole*—dominates the chamber, not only because it lacks competition from other decoration, but also because of the largeness of Russell's pictorial idea and the strength and vitality of its expression.

brought the action into the visual space of the assembly. By relegating Lewis and Clark to the quiet of the middle ground at right, Russell gives over the most important part of the picture space to Montana's original inhabitants. Nowhere else in the Capitol is the Indian presence in Montana so celebrated.

The Capitol painting by Russell is recognized as one of the best paintings he ever did. It has achieved national renown—because of Russell's eventual fame as the quintessential western artist, of course, but also because of the genuine artistic achievement that it represents. For someone who was a stranger to public art, Russell used the raw materials of artistic production in powerful ways to create a work about the history of Montana that touched the emotions of the public directly and profoundly.

Charles M. Russell. *Lewis and Clark Meeting Indians at Ross' Hole,* 1912. Oil on canvas, 140"×296". House Chamber

Lewis and Clark Meeting the Indians at Ross' Hole imagines the rituals enacted at that most significant encounter. In the right mid-ground, the Shoshone interpreter Old Toby communicates by sign language with a Salish leader (presumably Chief Three Eagles) while Lewis (left) and Clark (right) observe with care. In a gesture of lavish hospitality, a young warrior spreads white buffalo robes on the grass for the visitors. Sacagawea kneels at the right with her tiny son strapped to her back, watching attentively, while mounted warriors dash in from the encampment at the upper left. The Bitterroot Mountains, already topped with snow, stand like brooding sentinels, as if to warn the explorers of the challenge awaiting them.

67

Ralph Earll DeCamp (1858–1936)

ALMOST HIDDEN AWAY in the Old Law Library on the third floor are ten large landscapes. High above eye level, decorating the upper reaches of the chamber, they portray picturesque sites in Montana with grace and dignity. The paintings are the work of the third member of the triumvirate of Montana artists to create paintings for the Capitol expansion in 1911–12: Ralph Earll DeCamp. Painted for what was originally the Law Library, DeCamp's landscapes invite the question: Why landscapes for a state capitol, and particularly for its law library? The State Capitol of Pennsylvania, for example, boasted history paintings in its Supreme Court chamber that illustrated the power of the law in famous episodes from the past.

Perhaps the Capitol Commission contracted with a landscape artist because they wanted to provide a contemplative visual environment. Possibly its members were inspired by the distinguished tradition of western landscape painting by such outstanding artists as Albert Bierstadt and Thomas Moran, some of whose greatest works hung on the walls of the Capitol of the United States in Washington, D.C. The network between nature, the railroads, tourism, and art that developed in the late nineteenth century must also be considered a factor. To advance their economic agenda, the transcontinental railroads had made astute use of western landscape artists—including DeCamp himself, who produced paintings of Yellowstone National Park for the Northern Pacific Railroad early in his career.

Paramount as a reason, however, had to be the Montana landscape itself. Each state has physical features and historic landscapes dear to its citizens, but some states have landscapes so extraordinary as to become nationally famous. Such was Montana—abounding in aesthetically pleasing mountain vistas, natural wonders, and land that produced mineral wealth, timber, and agricultural bounty. And in 1911 Montanans were becoming increasingly aware not only of their mineral wealth but the commercial potential of tourism. John Raftery of Helena, editor of *The Treasure State*, argued forcefully in those pages in 1910 that Montana's "scenic wonders" could be turned into a "priceless asset." Perhaps the choice of a landscape motif—subject matter that expressed transcendent meaning at the same time that it subtly suggested commercial value—was a response to such cultural currents.

On the other hand, the choice of landscapes simply may have derived from the need to find a qualified Montana painter, for it is not clear if the Commission set out to hire a landscape painter or to obtain the services of a qualified Montana artist who, it so happened, painted landscapes. In either case, the Capitol Commission did not have to look far to find its man. Ralph DeCamp lived and worked in Helena. Never economically free to paint full-time, he

This photograph of Ralph E. DeCamp and Charles M. Russell, circa 1910, documents the camaraderie shared by the three Montana Capitol artists. While not close friends, each thought well of the other two, both personally and professionally.

served as a draftsman for the United States Surveyor General's Office from 1896 until his retirement in 1924 and prior to that as manager of the Helena Abstract and Title Company. Art was his true vocation, however, something he had practiced since his teenage years in Minnesota. By 1911, he had earned high marks in Montana for the quality of his landscape paintings.

Born in Attica, New York, in 1858, DeCamp moved with his family in the late 1860s to the Milwaukee area, where he received his first instruction in art. He established himself as an artist while yet in his teens when he moved once again with his family to Minnesota (first Oak Lake, subsequently Moorhead), although he supported himself through work in a variety of occupations relating to steamboating, the lumber industry, and even threshing. Encouraged to pursue formal training, he apparently set off

to study in Philadelphia in fall 1881, perhaps at the Pennsylvania Academy of the Fine Arts.

DeCamp was introduced to the West by Charles Fee, general passenger and ticket agent for the Northern Pacific Railroad, who had discovered his work. (Fee had also served as the intermediary between Governor Toole and the Northern Pacific concerning the services of Amédée Joullin in 1902–3). After a brief stint working as an artist for the Northern Pacific, DeCamp moved to Helena and forged ahead with dual careers in business/government and art. His wife, Margaret Hilger, was an accomplished violinist, and together they made a notable contribution to the cultural life of Helena.

After moving to Helena in 1886, DeCamp exhibited his paintings at such prestigious venues as the 1893 World's Columbian Exposition in Chicago and a national exhibition in San

Ralph E. DeCamp. *The Gallatin,* 1912. Oil on canvas, 42"×83". Old Law Library

The Gallatin refers to the area of southern Montana immediately north of Yellowstone National Park through which the Gallatin River (pictured) flows. Once again, DeCamp chose a spot from which one sees water, mountains, and big sky at the same time. The river in this case is centered, flowing gently toward the viewer. The artist seems to enjoy playing the curve of the tree-lined river against the encircling contour of mountain behind it.

Antonio in 1907. Locally, he presided over an artists' sketch club in Helena (which included Russell for a brief period). He was also a very talented photographer. Unlike either Russell or Paxson—both of whom he knew, sometimes exhibited with, and even occasionally collaborated with—DeCamp's artistic reputation never really extended beyond Montana.

In 1911, DeCamp was authorized to paint six murals for the Law Library. The result was the creation of *The Bitter Root, Last Chance, St. Ignatius (Indian Country), The Gallatin, Gates of the Mountains,* and *Lake McDermott.* In 1927, the legislature directed the State Board of Examiners to commission four more murals from DeCamp, thus completing the painting cycle for the Capitol: *Holter Dam, The Flathead, Above Timberline,* and *The Rosebud River.* DeCamp received eighteen hundred dollars for the original commission and sixteen hundred (one hundred more per painting) for the second round. The ten paintings represent a coherent group, painted with equal facility and in the same style.

DeCamp's site choices (which were his to make, although subject to official veto) emphasized mountain and water views, usually in conjunction. Politics naturally found its way into the discussion surrounding the murals, with each section of the state clamoring to be represented on the walls of the Capitol. That did not happen. Government rhetoric to the contrary, DeCamp offered a variety of mountain scenery, primarily from western and south-central Montana, and ignored the prairie east. The Bitterroot, Flathead, and Glacier scenes are western. *Above Timberline, The Gallatin,* and *The Rosebud River* represent the mountainous south. Three of the sites

Ralph E. DeCamp. *Gates of the Mountains,* 1911. Oil on canvas, 42"×83". Old Law Library

DeCamp reduces the bright colors used by the Pedrettis in their rendition of the same general area in order to achieve a softer, more autumnal look. The gates-like effect of the geological formation (so poetically named by Meriwether Lewis in 1805) is difficult to capture in photographs or paintings. DeCamp sought to overcome the difficulty by compositional means (the sidelong view of the Missouri River issuing from the narrow space between the cliffs) and by the manipulation of light and tone (distinguishing subtly but convincingly between the opposing cliffs).

are located in or near Helena: *Last Chance, Gates of the Mountains,* and *Holter Dam.*

DeCamp departed from his usual preference for pure landscape by showing the human use of natural resources in *Last Chance* and *Holter Dam,* thus extolling the concept of power over nature and modern methods of achieving it. This message is counterbalanced in the pastoral values espoused in *St. Ignatius (Indian Country)*, where nature and humankind are shown in harmony.

Overall, the ten paintings are elegiac in mood, presenting a gentle, nonthreatening view of Montana scenery, even of remote wilderness sites. Lakes lie placid, rivers ply their ways calmly under the benign watchfulness of tall mountains. Even the pent-up water hurling over Holter Dam takes up only a small part of the picture space in an otherwise dreamlike view. Only the Rosebud gushes with force, projecting itself into the very space of the viewer. In resisting the temptation to overdramatize, DeCamp distinguishes himself from the heroic landscape tradition of Albert Bierstadt and even from the technicolor wonders of his fellow western artist John Fery. The lyric, almost tender feeling DeCamp brings to Montana scenery is implemented by delicate colors softly applied: the lightly inflected grays of mountain masses, the sweetened dots of yellow indicating aspen leaves in autumn. By proclaiming the glories of the Montana landscape in a quiet voice, DeCamp made it possible for all to hear who listen well.

Ralph E. DeCamp. *Last Chance*, 1911. Oil on canvas, 42"×83". Old Law Library

One of only two landscapes that depict the use of the land for industrial purposes, *Last Chance* returns the Helena area to its pre-urban setting when placer miners originally looked for gold in the Helena Valley. For all his emphasis on the geographical context, most notably Mount Helena towering in the distance, DeCamp does not stint on practical details. The miner closest to the viewer expertly directs the full force of a hydraulic stream as his cohorts work in the background. The predominance of brown tones differentiates this painting from all the others, rendering its effect less decorative.

The photograph above, likely taken by DeCamp himself on the outskirts of Helena, served as the basis for the painting *Last Chance*. An accomplished photographer, DeCamp took many pictures of Montana scenery, some of which he used as visual aids in producing paintings of the same sites. DeCamp made subtle changes in the painting: he shifted the viewpoint so that the viewer is looking down on the scene, placed the figures farther into the distance, integrated the machinery at the left more thoughtfully into the composition, and gave more emphasis to the surrounding area.

Ralph E. DeCamp. *St. Ignatius (Indian Country),* 1911. Oil on canvas, 42"×83". Old Law Library

The title refers to the Jesuit mission of St. Ignatius founded in the foothills of the Mission Mountains in the nineteenth century—although the mission itself is not visible in the painting. The old-fashioned appellation "Indian Country" used by DeCamp refers to the fact that St. Ignatius was then (and continues to be) part of the Flathead Indian Reservation. DeCamp depicts a scene reminiscent of the pre-encounter period, before the influx of white settlers: Native Americans living on successful and peaceful terms with nature.

Ralph E. DeCamp. *Lake McDermott,* 1912. Oil on canvas, 42"×83". Old Law Library

A small body of water that feeds larger Lake Sherburne, Lake McDermott (now known as Swiftcurrent Lake) is located near the Grinnell Glacier in the eastern part of Glacier National Park. An acclaimed tourist destination by 1912, this portion of the northern Rocky Mountains became a national park in 1910. In this painting, DeCamp uses snow to highlight the surrounding mountains and draw attention to the geophysical features of glaciation.

Ralph E. DeCamp. *Above Timberline,* 1928. Oil on canvas, 42"×83". Old Law Library

Above Timberline is the only one of the ten landscape paintings that does not allude to a specific site in its title, although the scene is thought to be one from the Granite Range near the northeastern part of Yellowstone National Park. Trees are noticeably absent, and the craggy peaks are expressive of a colder, loftier elevation.

Ralph E. DeCamp. *The Rosebud River*, 1928. Oil on canvas, 42"×83". Old Law Library

The most turbulent of all of DeCamp's water scenes, *The Rosebud River* perhaps succeeds best in expressing the starkness, solitary beauty, and potential violence of wilderness Montana. The exact site is thought to be just above East Rosebud Lake, west of Red Lodge. Even today, the spot is difficult to access, further confirming the personal quest each site represented to the artist.

Ralph E. DeCamp. *Holter Dam*, 1928. Oil on canvas, 42"×83". Old Law Library

By choosing a majestic panoramic view and situating the viewer on a high vantage point overlooking the dam in the distance, DeCamp pays homage to the beauty of the landscape while at the same time depicting with care details of one of the finest hydroelectric plants in the country. Holter Dam is located on the Missouri River near Wolf Creek, about forty miles north of Helena.

Ralph E. DeCamp. *The Flathead*, 1928. Oil on canvas, 42"×83". Old Law Library

DeCamp depicts Flathead Lake, one of the largest freshwater lakes in the country, in its pristine state. Human habitation is subtly indicated by the presence of Indian tepees in the right foreground. The large evergreen on the right not only serves as a visual reminder of the state's flora, but serves compositionally as a repoussoir, or framing device, within the picture.

THE
SCULPTURE

SUSAN R. NEAR

WHILE THE PAINTINGS on the Capitol walls were chosen to celebrate Montana history and depict the significance of democratic government, the building's sculptures serve a different purpose. Except for the allegorical figure of Lady Liberty, who stands high atop the Capitol Dome, the sculptures honor noteworthy politicians who made important contributions to Montana and the nation.

Unlike the Capitol murals, which were chosen by commissions responsible for the Capitol construction and expansion projects, most of the sculptures owe their placement primarily to citizen groups determined to honor specific individuals. Such groups would propose a memorial to the legislature, which would deliberate and often amend the proposal before issuing approval. For the most part, the responsibility for paying for the tribute was left to the private sector.

Those whose likenesses are preserved in the Capitol in bronze and marble have this in common: they had a constituency who believed them worthy of such a public monument; their reputations were such that the legislature agreed to allow a memorial on the Capitol grounds; and their constituency had adequate access to resources—in other words, was able to raise money for the project within the time constraints set by the legislature. Raising money and hiring an artist to create a successful memorial was no easy task, and not all projects authorized by the legislature for display in the Capitol came to fruition. Among those that did not are a statue of Fred Whiteside, the Flathead County legislator who exposed the corruption of the first Capitol Commission, and a monument to honor the state's American Indian communities, which was to have included a Montana tribal flag circle.

Thus, Montana has honored important political leaders by permanently placing statues of them in the Capitol—but sparingly over a century. The subjects all played significant roles on the national and/or international scene—representing what is best of Montana in the process.

A large crowd gathered for the 1905 dedication of the statue of Acting Territorial Governor Thomas Francis Meagher.

The sculptures themselves range in size and prominence from the heroic bronzes of Acting Territorial Governor Thomas Francis Meagher, Senator Wilbur Fisk Sanders, Congresswoman Jeannette Rankin, and Senator Mike Mansfield and his wife Maureen, to the more modest busts of Senator Thomas J. Walsh, Senator Burton K. Wheeler, and Governor Joseph M. Dixon.

The size of the sculpture certainly does not reflect the merit of the individual honored or his or her contributions. Rather, it seems to reflect the times in which the memorial was championed. Early commemorations tended to be larger than life. The sculptures of Thomas Francis Meagher, dedicated in 1905, and of Wilbur Fisk Sanders, dedicated in 1913, were both commissioned during the Progressive Era.

The decision to commission small busts of Walsh, Dixon, and Wheeler perhaps can be attributed to the availability of space in the niches of the Rotunda, but the more modest tributes also fit with the tenor of their times—whether the depression years of the 1930s, in the case of Walsh, or the idealistic 1970s, when many wished for a more egalitarian society, in the cases of Dixon and Wheeler. An exception is the monumental bronze of Jeannette Rankin, erected in 1980. Her symbolic significance as the first woman elected to Congress seemed to call for something big. In 2001, the dedication of the heroic-size Mike and Maureen Mansfield sculpture suggests that once again Montanans hunger for exemplars of public service who are larger than life.

Liberty

STANDING PROMINENTLY ABOVE Montana's Capitol, Lady Liberty holds a torch and a shield to light the way and protect the populace. The allegorical *Liberty* fits well with the Capitol's neoclassical architecture. As a relatively new state in 1901, Montana wished to announce to all its commitment to American political culture. Thus, the commissioning of *Liberty* represented a visual expression of Montana's dedication to the traditions of democracy.

Ironically, this very public symbol of democracy in Montana was selected and procured by the first Capitol Commission, which disbanded amidst a corruption scandal. Any records concerning the purchase of the statue or the selection or name of the artist disappeared with the Commission.

Montana's *Liberty* differs markedly from the famous Statue of Liberty in the New York harbor, but some have recognized parallel features in one of the sculptures adorning the Supreme Court building in Washington, D.C. What is known about the sculpture comes from newspaper accounts. The Capitol's statue appeared, crated, at the Northern Pacific depot in Helena and was delivered to the Capitol for placement under the direction of the second Capitol Commission. It was installed atop the Capitol Dome on September 15, 1901.

Artist unknown. *Liberty*, circa 1900. Copper sheeting over iron framework, by an unknown Ohio foundry, 144"×42"×36". Atop the Capitol Dome. This photograph of *Liberty* was taken in 1934, as workers employed by the Civil Works Administration, including the man in the lower right, resheeted the Capitol Dome with copper.

Thomas Francis Meagher

THOMAS FRANCIS MEAGHER (1823–1867) was an Irish revolutionary, flamboyant orator, and Union veteran of the Civil War who twice served as acting governor of Montana Territory. Exiled from the British Isles to a penal colony in Tasmania in 1848, this Irish freedom fighter soon escaped to New York City. Arriving in Montana in 1865 at the height of its gold rush, Meagher served as acting territorial governor in 1865–66 and 1866–67. His political terms are viewed by many as opportunistic and corrupt. Meagher's mysterious disappearance from a steamboat in 1867 has led to disparate theories about the cause of his death—from falling into the Missouri River while intoxicated to premeditated murder by British agents.

More than for any direct contribution to Montana, Thomas Francis Meagher owes his place on the Capitol grounds to his Irish Catholic heritage and Irish nationalist politics. Protestant Irish, or "Orangemen," led Helena's 1894 bid for the capital, while Irish Catholics led by copper magnate Marcus Daly favored Anaconda. Though Helena won the capital fight, in 1905 Anaconda backers settled the score. The Meagher Memorial Association raised twenty thousand dollars by public subscription for the statue by Irish-born Chicago sculptor Charles J. Mulligan (1866–1916). On July 4, 1905, speakers extolled Meagher's love of liberty and Irish heritage as his statue was dedicated before a crowd of over fifteen hundred.

Charles J. Mulligan. *Thomas Francis Meagher*, 1905. Bronze, cast by the American Bronze Foundry, Chicago, 108"×72"×36".
Granite pedestal designed by Charles Lane and constructed by James Welch and Company, Butte, 120"×153"×81". North Lawn

Wilbur Fisk Sanders

WILBUR FISK SANDERS (1834–1905) arrived in Bannack, Idaho Territory, in 1863 with his uncle Sidney Edgerton, the newly appointed chief justice of the territory. A lawyer, a Mason, and a Union veteran of the Civil War, Sanders is best remembered as an early prosecuting attorney and one of the organizers of the Vigilantes. Inscribed at the base of his statue is "Men Do Your Duty," the words used to order the hanging of road agent George Ives, prosecuted by Sanders and convicted of murder by a miners' court in 1863.

Keenly aware of the need to document Montana's early history, Sanders helped found the Historical Society of Montana in 1865, the year after Montana Territory was established. A perennially unsuccessful candidate for territorial representative, Sanders became one of Montana's first United States senators in 1889 by vote of the Montana legislature.

Soon after his death in 1905, Sanders's friends formed the Sanders Memorial Association. In what would become an unusual gesture, the 1911 legislative session appropriated five thousand dollars to erect his statue in the Montana Capitol Rotunda. Montana senator and copper baron William A. Clark provided free casting of the sculpture by Norwegian-born Chicago artist Sigvald Asbjornsen (b. 1867). The sculpture was cast at the Henry-Bonnard Bronze Company in Mount Vernon, New York; owned by Clark, it was the largest bronze works in the country.

Sigvald Asbjornsen. *Wilbur Fisk Sanders*, 1913. Bronze, cast by the Henry-Bonnard Bronze Company, Mount Vernon, New York, 131"×71"×68". Location to be determined

Thomas J. Walsh

WISCONSIN NATIVE Thomas J. Walsh (1859–1933) came to Helena, Montana, in 1890 to practice law. Walsh, whose diligence, thoroughness, and integrity were well respected, became Montana's senator in 1911 at age fifty-three. He served in the United States Senate for twenty-two years. Known as a lawyer's lawyer of unimpeachable character, Walsh championed women's suffrage, election reform, a progressive income tax, and laws to protect worker safety.

An outspoken liberal, Walsh became nationally prominent in 1924 when he led the investigation into corruption in the Warren G. Harding administration, exposing the Teapot Dome scandal—the illegal leases of naval oil reserves near Teapot Dome, Wyoming, and Elk Hill, California. Appointed United States Attorney General in 1933 by President Herbert Hoover, Walsh died en route to Washington, D.C., to assume the office. Sculpted by Louise K. Sparrow (1884–1979), the white marble bust of Senator Thomas J. Walsh was dedicated in 1930. Its placement in Montana's Capitol Rotunda coincided with his last reelection to the United States Senate.

Louise K. Sparrow. *Thomas J. Walsh*, 1930. Marble, 29"×21"×12". Rotunda

Joseph M. Dixon

In 1891, North Carolina native Joseph M. Dixon (1867–1934) moved to Missoula, Montana, where he quickly entered politics. He served as Montana's United States representative from 1903 to 1907 and as a senator from 1907 to 1913. An advocate of railroad regulation, mining-law reform, and a graduated income tax, Dixon's most memorable achievement was changing Montana's tax code so that mining companies paid their fair share of taxes. He effected this change by sponsoring an initiative during his term as governor (1921–25). The tax reform initiative passed by public vote but effectively ended Dixon's political career by earning him the steadfast enmity of the powerful Anaconda Copper Mining Company. His experience wrestling with the Company convinced Dixon that "the great handicap to real representative government . . . is the ease with which the great corporate interest can control [political] conventions and legislatures."

"It is high time indeed that this notable Montana governor be honored," the legislature declared in its authorization for a memorial to Joseph M. Dixon in 1971. The Dixon Memorial Committee raised funds to have Dixon's likeness in bronze cast by John W. Weaver (b. 1920), a Montana-born sculptor living in Canada. The memorial was dedicated in November 1972.

John W. Weaver. *Joseph M. Dixon*, 1972. Bronze, cast by a Canadian foundry, 28"×15"×11". Rotunda

Burton K. Wheeler

Afiery opponent of the Anaconda Copper Mining Company, attorney Burton K. Wheeler (1882–1975) began his political career as a state representative from Silver Bow County. During the difficult World War I era, the Massachusetts native became known as a champion of civil liberties for his refusal to prosecute alleged spies and saboteurs on the basis of rumor. Wheeler's steadfast support for First Amendment rights in the face of war-induced hysteria earned him the nickname "Bolshevik Burt" and lost him his position as United States district attorney.

Elected to the United States Senate in 1922, Wheeler served continuously from 1923 to 1947. In 1924, Wheeler campaigned against "the control of government and industry by private monopoly" when he ran for vice president on the Progressive Party ticket. In 1934, Wheeler sponsored the Indian Reorganization Act (the Wheeler-Howard Act), part of President Franklin Delano Roosevelt's New Deal legislation, that acknowledged Native American rights, established the framework for tribal self-governance, and ended the disastrous system of land allotment. Though once a staunch supporter of Roosevelt, Wheeler broke with the president over military aid to the Allies in the 1930s and Roosevelt's "court packing" scheme.

In 1977, two years after Wheeler's death, the legislature approved the placement of a memorial sculpture at the Capitol. The Greater Montana Foundation, which bore the cost of the project, quickly commissioned Browning artist Bob Scriver (1914–1999) to sculpt a likeness, and Wheeler's bust was installed in the Capitol Rotunda that same year. The inscription on the bronze reads, "Champion of Montana and its people, civil liberties, an independent supreme court and a noninterventionist foreign policy."

Robert M. Scriver. *Burton K. Wheeler*, 1977. Bronze, cast by Arrowhead Bronze Foundry, Kalispell, Montana, 30"×19"×12". Rotunda

Jeannette Rankin

Born near Missoula in Montana Territory, Jeannette Rankin (1880–1973) was a passionate proponent of world peace and women's rights. From 1910 through 1914, Rankin worked full time for women's suffrage, including in successful campaigns in Washington, California, and Montana. Montanans elected Rankin to represent them in the United States House of Representatives in 1916, making her the first woman democratically elected to any national legislative body. "I cannot vote for war," inscribed on the base of her statue in the Montana Capitol, are the words Rankin used as she cast her vote against America's entry into World War I in 1917. In 1940, Montanans again elected Rankin to the United States House, and in 1941, she cast the lone dissenting vote against the United States' entrance into World War II.

The Jeannette Rankin statue, created by twenty-five-year-old Montana native Terri Mimnaugh (b. 1955) and dedicated in 1980, depicts Rankin as she would have looked on her first day in Congress on April 1, 1917. Mimnaugh placed a document in Rankin's hands with the inscription, "When in one hundred years from now, courage, sheer courage based on moral indignation is celebrated in this country, the name of Jeannette Rankin, who stood firm in folly for her faith will be written in monumental bronze, not for what she did, but for the way she did it." These are the words of newspaper editor William Allan White after Rankin's vote against war in 1941.

Rankin's family donated most of the forty thousand dollars needed for the statue with some funds provided by the legislature. On May 1, 1985, a second casting of this monumental bronze was dedicated in the United States Capitol. It now represents Montana in the National Statuary Hall Collection along with a bronze of artist Charles M. Russell.

Terri Mimnaugh. *Jeannette Rankin*, 1980. Bronze, cast by Frontier Bronze, Great Falls, Montana, 100"×29"×29". Second-floor landing of the Grand Stairway

Mike and Maureen Mansfield

REVERED STATESMAN Mike Mansfield (1903–2001) served in government for nearly fifty years as a United States congressman, senator, and ambassador to Japan. A quiet, thoughtful man, Mansfield's most pronounced qualities were his even-handedness and the respect with which he treated both colleagues and constituents.

After growing up in Great Falls, Mansfield joined the United States Navy during World War I at the age of fourteen. Following his military service that included stints in the army and marine corps, Mansfield worked in the Butte mines. In Butte, he met high school teacher Maureen Hayes (1905–2000), who encouraged him to complete his education. The two married in 1932. Mansfield eventually earned a master's degree in history and political science from Montana State University in Missoula, where he taught until his election to Congress in 1942.

Mansfield served five consecutive terms in the United States House, before running for and winning a seat in the United States Senate, which he held from 1952 until his retirement from the Senate in 1977. From 1977 to 1989, he served as United States ambassador to Japan. As Senate majority leader, a position he held longer than any other person, Mansfield was instrumental in the passage of Civil Rights legislation, ratification of the nuclear test ban treaty, and United States diplomatic recognition of China. He was awarded the Presidential Medal of Freedom in 1989.

In 1999, a bipartisan group of Montanans formed to raise eighty thousand dollars for a monument to Mike Mansfield, an honor Mansfield refused to consider unless the monument also recognized his wife Maureen for her role in his success. After the legislature authorized placement of a statue, Fortine, Montana, native Gareth Curtiss (b. 1959) was chosen through a competition to create the monument, which was formally dedicated on November 26, 2001, a year after Maureen's and just weeks after Mike Mansfield's death.

Gareth Curtiss. *Mike and Maureen Mansfield*, 2001. Bronze, cast by the artist in Olympia, Washington, 102"×42"×30". South balcony of the third floor

ILLUSTRATIONS

SELECTED BIBLIOGRAPHY

Burnham, Patricia M. "Russell and the Capitol Mural." *Russell's West* 3, 1 (1995): 3–7.

"Laying the Cornerstone of the Capitol" and "The Dedication Ceremonies." In *Contributions to the Historical Society of Montana*. Vol. 4. Helena: Montana Historical Society, 1903.

Goodsell, Charles T. *The American Statehouse: Interpreting Democracy's Temples*. Lawrence: University Press of Kansas, 2000.

Hitchcock, Henry-Russell, and William Seale. *Temples of Democracy: The State Capitols of the USA*. New York: Harcourt Brace Jovanovich, 1976.

Lambert, Kirby. "Through the Artist's Eye: The Paintings and Photographs of R. E. DeCamp," *Montana The Magazine of Western History* 46 (Summer 1999): 42–55.

McDonald, James P. *Historic Structure Report: Montana State Capitol Building*. Helena: State of Montana, Architectural/Engineering Office, 1981.

Minutes of the State Furnishing Board. RS 201, Volume 3, Montana Historical Society Archives, Helena.

Owens, Kenneth N. "The Prizes of Statehood." *Montana The Magazine of Western History* 37 (Autumn 1987): 2–9.

"A Pulpit Orator: Rev. J. H. Crooker on the Capital/ An Eloquent Address at the Harvest Festival." Women's Helena for the Capital Club, 1894.

Records of the Capitol Commission. RS 65. Montana Historical Society Archives.

Taliaferro, John. *Charles M. Russell: The Life and Legend of America's Cowboy Artist*. Boston: Little, Brown and Company, 1996.

Van West, Carroll. "A Landscape of Statehood: The Montana State Capitol." *Montana The Magazine of Western History* 37 (Autumn 1987): 73–75.

Wilson, Richard Guy, Dianne H. Pilgrim, and Richard N. Murray. *The American Renaissance, 1876–1917*. New York: The Brooklyn Museum, 1979.

INDEX

ABOUT THE AUTHORS

Kirby Lambert has been the Curator of Collections for the Montana Historical Society since 1989. A native of Texas, he received his master of arts degree in museum studies from Texas Tech University in Lubbock before moving to Helena in 1985. As curator of Montana's museum he helps care for and interpret the state's most notable treasures, including the art in the State Capitol. Lambert has researched a wide variety of topics related to the museum's collections and is a regular contributor to *Montana The Magazine of Western History* and other periodicals. He is the compiler of *Charlie Russell Journal* (Helena: Montana Historical Society Press, 1997), a light-hearted chronicle of the "Cowboy Artist's" observances in word and picture.

Born and raised in New England, **Patricia M. Burnham** received a doctorate in art history at Boston University in 1984, specializing in American art. For the past ten years, her research has focused on American history painting. In 1995, Cambridge University Press published *Redefining American History Painting*, a volume of essays she co-edited with Lucretia Giese. It was her interest in history painting that prompted her to make the Capitol murals of Montana the subject of her recent studies. Dr. Burnham now lives in Austin, Texas, where she teaches in the American Studies program and the Department of Art and Art History at the University of Texas.

After receiving a master's degree in American history from the University of Delaware in 1981, **Susan R. Near** joined the staff of the Montana Historical Society. Director of Museum Services since 1989, Near is responsible for the curatorial activities, exhibitions, and educational programs for Montana's Museum, the Original Governor's Mansion, and the Montana State Capitol. She has been curator for over twenty major exhibitions—including ones featuring Capitol artists Charles M. Russell and Edgar Paxson. Near played a significant role in the recent Capitol renovation project, for which she served as the state's fine-art consultant.